EAST ANGLIAN ARCHAEOLOGY

Frontispiece: Aerial view of excavation

A Late Neolithic, Saxon and Medieval Site at Middle Harling, Norfolk

by Andrew Rogerson

with contributions by
Marion Archibald, Justine Bayley,
John Cherry, Catherine Coutts,
Carol Cunningham, Paul Drury,
Francis Healy, Kathy Kilmurry,
Sue Margeson and Rosemary Powers

illustrations by
Steven Ashley

and photographs by
David Wicks

East Anglian Archaeology
Report No. 74, 1995

The British Museum

Field Archaeology Division
Norfolk Museums Service

EAST ANGLIAN ARCHAEOLOGY
REPORT NO. 74

Published by
The British Museum
London WC1B 3DG
and
Field Archaeology Division
Norfolk Museums Service
Union House
Gressenhall
Dereham
Norfolk NR20 4DR

in conjunction with
The Scole Archaeological Committee

Editor: Peter Wade-Martins
EAA Managing Editor: Jenny Glazebrook

Scole Editorial sub-committee:
David Buckley, County Archaeologist, Essex Planning Department
Keith Wade, County Archaeological Officer, Suffolk Planning Department
Peter Wade-Martins, County Field Archaeologist, Norfolk Museums Service
Stanley West

Set in Times Roman by Joan Daniells using ® Ventura Publisher
Printed by Geerings of Ashford Ltd., Ashford, Kent

ISBN 0 905594 17 7

For details of *East Anglian Archaeology,* see inside front cover

Cover illustration:
Group of representative coins from the Middle Harling hoard
(*copyright British Museum, by kind permission of the Trustees*)

Contents

List of Plates

List of Figures

List of Tables

Contents of Microfiche

Contributors

Marion M. Archibald, M.A., F.S.A., F.M.A.,
Assistant Keeper, Department of Coins and Medals,
British Museum

Steven Ashley, F.C.S.D., A.I.F.A.,
Illustrator, Norfolk Archaeological Unit

Justine Bayley, M.Sc., MSc.,
Head of Technology Branch, Ancient Monuments
Laboratory

John Cherry, M.A., F.S.A.,
Deputy Keeper, Department of Medieval and Later
Antiquities, British Museum

Catherine M. Coutts, B.A., F.S.A. (Scot.),
Archaeological Field Officer, British School at Rome

Carol Cunningham

Paul Drury, A.R.I.C.S., F.S.A.,
Director, London Region Conservation Group, English
Heritage

Frances Healy, B.Sc. (Econ.), Ph.D., F.S.A., M.I.F.A.,
Senior Research Officer, Oxford Archaeological Unit

John Hostler,
formerly Illustrator, Norfolk Archaeological Unit

Kathy Kilmurry, Ph.D.

Sue Margeson, Ph.D., F.S.A., A.M.A.,
Keeper of Archaeology, Norwich Castle Museum

Rosemary Powers,
formerly Higher Scientific Officer, Human Origins
Group, British Museum (Natural History)

Andrew Rogerson, B.A., F.S.A., M.I.F.A.,
Senior Landscape Archaeologist, Norfolk Museums
Service

Acknowledgements

I am grateful to the landowner, Mr Richard Barker, for permission to excavate, and to the Trustees of the British Museum for their generous funding of the project. I would also like to thank the following: Leslie Webster and John Cherry for all their help and encouragement; Marion Archibald for her enthusiastic and expert advice in the pursuit of Beonnas; Tony and Henry Frost who wielded their metal detectors with such skill in every weather condition; Barbara Green, Sue Margeson and Bill Milligan of Norwich Castle Museum for their staunch support before, during, and after the excavation; David Bailey for his prompt reporting of coins and other finds; Alan Davison who first brought the site to my attention and later helped with matters historical; Steven Ashley who drew the field plans and most of the published drawings; David Wicks, site and finds photographer; the excavation team which consisted of Andrew Bull, David Gill, Neville Guy, James Heathcote, and Mark Newton; Pattie Macadam of the British Museum (Natural History) who carefully excavated the contents of one post-medieval bone pit; my former colleagues John Wymer and the late Tony Gregory for their helpful guidance during site visits; and finally all the contributors, both major and minor, without whom this report could not have been written.

Frances Healy is grateful to Jeff Bock (Department of Mathematics and Computer Studies, Norwich City College of Further and Higher Education) for much patient help with the processing of lithic material, and to Stuart and Vera Friedenson for painstakingly washing and marking it. Particular thanks are due to R. V. Davis for the petrological identification of the stone axe fragment S1. Gillian Varndell has kindly made it possible to examine the Icklingham material in the British Museum. John Hostler drew the prehistoric artefacts. Rosamund Cleal, Ian Longworth, Bob Silvester, and John Wymer have commented on and induced some improvement in the text.

The report has been copyedited by Susie West, and indexed by Peter Gunn.

Summary

Excavation of part of a Middle Saxon rural settlement attempted to establish the context of a mid 8th-century coin hoard which had been found scattered in the ploughsoil and below. The hoard had probably been buried in a location peripheral to the main zone of contemporary activity the extent of which is known from a surface scatter of finds. Occupation within the excavated area continued into the early 13th century. The Later Neolithic was evidenced by scattered pit groups. Prolific finds of coins and metalwork, predominantly Middle Saxon to medieval, from the excavation and the immediate surroundings are described.

Chapter 1. Introduction

I. The Physical Background
(Figs 1–3)

Middle Harling, once a separate settlement, is now represented by Middle Farm, a lodge to the former hall at West Harling, and a sparse sprinkling of cottages and bungalows. The excavated site, 11km east-north-east of Thetford and 25km north-east of Bury St Edmunds, is situated in the northern centre of the modern civil parish of Harling (which comprises an area of *c.* 2300 hectares). The excavation took place towards the west end of the present settlement of Middle Harling immediately south of a track leading to West Harling, and north of a copse named Church Clump which masks the site of St Andrew's Church. The track runs parallel to the southern edge of the valley floor of the River Thet (Figs 2 and 3). The flood plain is now a mixture of arable and pasture, and at this point is *c.* 0.9km wide, aligned roughly north-east to south-west. The Early Iron Age site of Micklemoor Hill sits on an island within the valley *c.* 0.8km north-west of the excavation. To the north-east beyond Middle Farm a short tributary valley runs north to the Thet and effectively demarks Middle Harling from the small town of East Harling, while to the south-west a less pronounced valley with low-lying peaty patches and localised hummocks

intervenes between Middle and West Harling, itself a now almost deserted settlement. The site sits close to the eastern edge of Breckland with sandy soils extending far to north, south and west, while medium and heavier soils lie *c.* 2.5km to the east. Bailey (1989, 35–6) categorised West Harling (which included Middle Harling) as a 'central' Breckland parish, with more than 50% of its land adjudged as Grade 4 or 5 by the Agricultural Land Classification Survey. East Harling, containing mainly Grade 3 land, fell into Bailey's 'peripheral' category. This distinction admirably demonstrates that Middle Harling was placed close to the division between zones of widely differing soils and distinct agro-economic and settlement histories. The excavated site lies on land of Grade 4 (ADAS/MAFF/SOIL SURVEY Map Sheet 135, 1972).

The surface of the area of excavation, at *c.* 19m OD, was fairly level, with a very slight dip in the south-east corner. The ploughed surface exhibited no significant soil marks and was a consistent, well-drained grey brown chalky loamy sand, apparently of the Methwold Series (Corbett 1973, 62–3). The natural subsoil was chalk-sand drift, consisting of areas of concreted chalk lumps and particles overlain in places by variably sized pockets of yellow brown sand with flints. The landscape is of the slope category, as distinguished by Murphy (1984, 15–7).

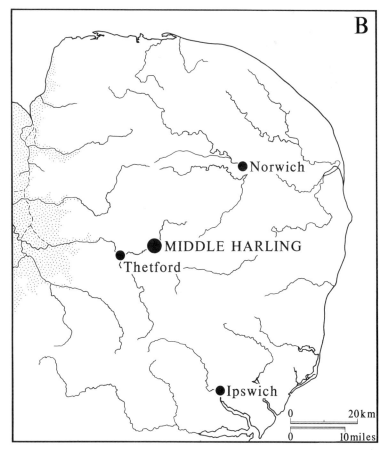

Figure 1 Location maps

II. The Historical Background

Harling, which in *Domesday* lay in the hundred of Guiltcross, was first recorded as *Herlingham* in a will of 1046 (Whitelock 1930, 84–5; Hart 1966, 92; Sawyer 1968, no. 1535), and slightly later as *Herlinge* (Whitelock 1930, 88–9; Hart 1966, 95; Sawyer 1968, no. 1519). The estate in question became one of two *Domesday* manors of East Harling. *Domesday* lists five manors in *Herlinga*, which have been assigned to East (two manors), West and Middle Harling, and Harling Thorpe (Davison 1980, 295). Blomefield (1805, 297–300) similarly assigned the manors, with the exception of one which he allotted to Harling Thorpe rather than East Harling. There is no doubt that the manor held by Ulfketel from Alan, Count of Brittany, was that of Middle Harling. The twenty-six (TRE) men of varying status there listed make up 39% of

the total of 66 men entered in the five combined manors. These figures indicate that Middle Harling was the most populous settlement in the 11th century. In addition the Middle Harling manor contained four carucates, and the other four manors only five in all.

In 1254 Middle Harling first appears by name as *Harling Media* (Davison 1980, 296). The settlement's importance had certainly declined by 1334 when the figure it paid (40/-) was the lowest sum in Guiltcross Hundred. By the early 15th century it had come into the ownership of the Berdewell family who also held West Harling. Thereafter, although Middle Harling retained some independence, its manorial and agricultural fortunes were closely bound up with those of its westerly neighbour. The rectory was consolidated with that of West Harling in the later 15th century, and the church was closed in 1543. There are no further signs of major decline until the first

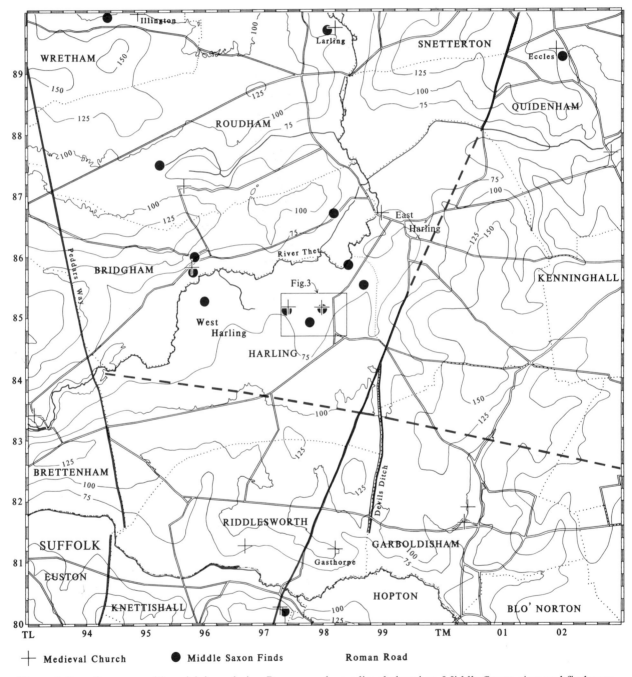

+ Medieval Church   ● Middle Saxon Finds   Roman Road

Figure 2 Location map, with parish boundaries, Roman roads, medieval churches, Middle Saxon sites and findspots, and contours at intervals of 25 feet.

2

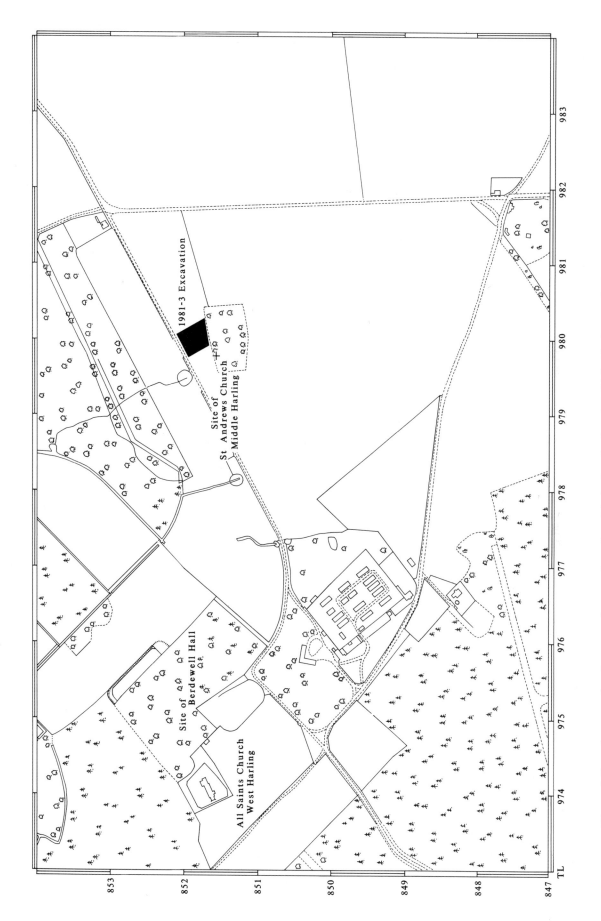

Figure 3 Location map showing area of excavation, site of St Andrew's church, Middle Harling, and All Saints', West Harling. Scale 1:5000.

3

four decades of the 18th century when large scale estate creation by the Draper, Gipps and Croftes families led to widespread depopulation in both Middle and West Harling.

A detailed account of the decline of these two along with Harling Thorpe may be found in Davison (1980) from which most of the above information is derived.

III. The Archaeological Background
(Figs 2–4)

The Roman and post-Roman settlement history of the former parish of West Harling has been well served by the recent work of Alan Davison (1980 and 1983). Site numbers cited below are those county numbers contained in the Norfolk Sites and Monuments Record. A Roman road (site 6116; Margary 1973, 331), a branch from the Peddars Way joining Stanton Chair (Suffolk) with Crownthorpe (Norfolk) cuts across Harling from south-south-west to north-north-east towards the eastern end of the parish. The Devil's Dyke, (site 6115), a badly mutilated linear earthwork, runs north from the Little Ouse valley, and consisted of a bank to the east and a ditch to the west, with an intermittent western counterscarp bank. Throughout its length the dyke was, or is, a parish boundary, and the northernmost stretch formed the division between East and West Harling. The earthwork meets the Roman road at an acute angle, and has not been recorded north of the road. However, its line is approximately continued by a stream flowing north to the River Thet. This watercourse was also the East/West Harling boundary. Just less than 3km in length the Dyke is now nowhere sufficiently large to appear defensive. It has not been excavated and remains undated.

A small Romano-British settlement (site 19223) lies about 100m west of West Harling Church at TL 9725 8513 (centre) and has produced pottery and coins of the 3rd and 4th centuries. A concentration of late 1st and 2nd-century pottery has recently been recorded at TL 9600 8513 (site 25339) west of Stonehouse Farm, West Harling. Another thick surface spread of early Roman sherds occurs south of the site of Middle Harling Church at TL 9795 8503 (site 6033).

No early Anglo-Saxon material has been recovered from the vicinity of the excavation apart from a small-long brooch at TL 9785 8509 (site 6033) and a possible wrist-clasp fragment at TL 9763 8507 (site 24662). With the exception of a coin of Aethelstan of East Anglia (c. 825) and of two Ipswich ware sherds found during intensive fieldwalking, Middle Saxon finds are absent from site 11803, the open ground immediately to the south and west of West Harling churchyard, although it has produced pottery of Late Saxon to early 18th-century date. A single sherd of Ipswich ware was found in a disturbed context during the digging of a trench in the southern part of the churchyard, in preparation for the reinternment of human bones from the 1982–3 excavations. Seven sherds of Ipswich ware on the Roman site (25339) probably indicate Middle Saxon settlement in West Harling over 1km from the parish church. North of this site, over the Thet, the village of Bridgham has yielded two areas of Middle Saxon finds (sites 17183 and 18066). Finds from the latter, which lies near the parish church, includes two sherds of Northern French Blackware. A penny of Cnut has been found at TL 9771 8507 (site 24454; Coin no. 85,

p.50), midway between Middle and West Harling churches, and a contemporary imitation of a Cnut penny to the south of the excavation at TL 9778 8495 (site 19762; coin no. 118, p.52). Middle Saxon Ipswich ware has been collected from the surface of three sites in Middle Harling at some distance from the excavation, at TL 9873 8550 (site 20040; two sherds), TL 9843 8586 (site 18454; one sherd) and TL 9780 8480 (site 16957; one sherd). None has been submitted to systematic fieldwalking, but it is unlikely that any are settlement sites of this date. Reference should also be made to Middle Saxon finds, 4.5km north of Middle Harling, in the strangely rhyming parish of Larling (civil parish of Roudham). Here the now isolated church of St Aethelbert stands adjacent to a field (site 6000) which has yielded a decorated whale-bone panel fragment of the late 8th century (Green 1971; Webster and Backhouse 1991, 179, cat. no. 139), as well as four sherds of Ipswich ware.

The deserted settlement of Harling Thorpe at TL 947 842 (site 6087) has yielded small quantities of medieval pottery but two pre-Conquest finds have been made nearby, a cut halfpenny of Harthacnut and a penny of Harold I (sites 23310 and 23505). In the extreme north-west of the old parish of West Harling a fragment of an Early Saxon square-headed brooch has been found on a Romano-British settlement at TL 943 838 (site 6060). This is probably a transpontine outlier of the substantial Romano-British settlement at Brettenham/Bridgham within which abundant evidence for an Early Saxon inhumation cemetery has been recovered.

Davison's (1983) work has shown the evidence for the pattern of medieval settlements in West Harling but additional discoveries add a little to the layout of Middle Harling. Surface concentrations of 13th and 14th-century pottery have been recorded at TL 9852 8584 and TL 9843 8586 (sites 19699 and 18454) on sandy hillocks in a field of peaty soil. Another site, yielding rather fewer sherds, has been located at TL 9820 8535 (site 18524). These three sites extend the settled area shown by Davison (1983, 331) north-east towards and beyond the present Middle Harling Farm. The field north of the excavation site (Fig. 4), site 6033 context 7, produced a substantial concentration of medieval finds, but over a more restricted area than is shown on Davison's plan (1983, 331). Despite the presence of some Middle and Late Saxon pottery, and indeed three Beonna pennies (s.f. 614, 652 and 653, Fig. 33), this site appears to have been occupied from the 13th to the late 15th or early 16th century. A number of important metalwork finds discovered by Tony Frost and David Bailey are published in this report. While conducting his fieldwork in 1980 Mr Davison collected Middle and Late Saxon and medieval sherds from the surface of the field that was soon to produce the Beonna coin hoard. Previous to these finds the only archaeological record referred to the ploughing up of human bones immediately north of Church Clump in 1970.

St Andrew's Church does not appear in *Domesday* and a priest is not recorded until 1308. The building was 'entirely taken down' in 1543, but Blomefield could still see the foundations in the 1730s (1805, 315). Within a few years, the lord of the manor, William Crofts, had indulged in an act of desecration and below ground demolition that outraged an anonymous 18th-century eye witness (Davison 1980, 303):

'Anno 17- Wm. Crofts Esq. in order to Improve his low adjoyning morasses and low meadows, carried away the whole foundations with the mortar & rubbish of Middle Harling Church & spread therupon. It was a shocking sight to see how indecently the Bones of the deceasd' persons who lay interrd there were humbled and scattered about. Who can promise quiet to himself in this world if we are to be thus disturb'd even in our graves. The church had been dilapidated many years before this: abt 40 yrs ago Sr Bassingbourn Gawdy Bart. gave me a large old rusty

key plough'd up in this church-yard which probably belonged to one of the locks of the church doors'. (N.R.O., Frere MSS 352 x 3, DS 594)

This destruction must have taken place shortly after 1743 when William Croftes succeeded to the estate and gained ownership of Middle Harling churchyard through exchange (Davison 1980, 303).

The land reclamation resulting from the desecration is apparent today on site 21025 (Fig. 4), which was

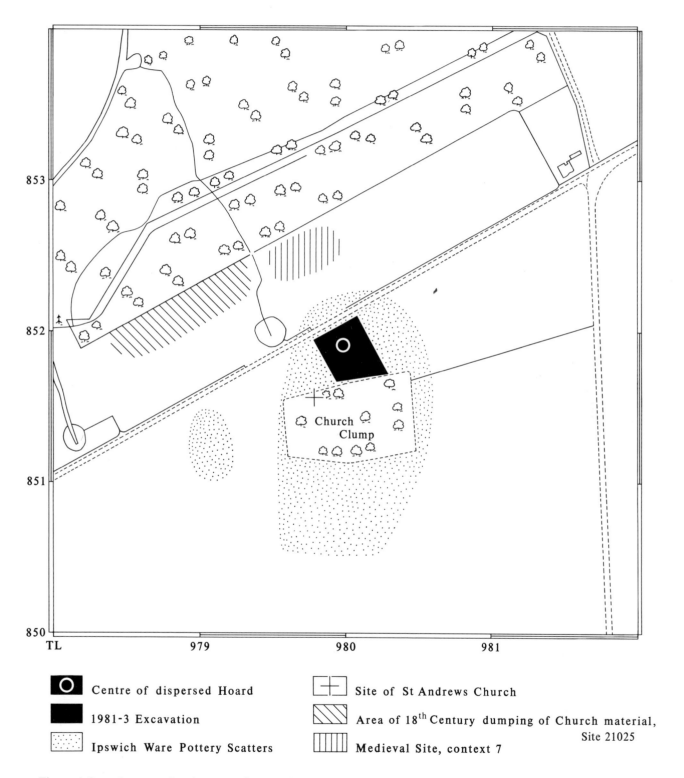

Figure 4 Location map showing area of excavation, site of Beonna hoard, area of Middle Saxon pottery scatter, area of dumping of church material site 21025, and medieval site, context 7. Scale 1:2500.

discovered in 1983 by Tony Frost of East Harling. The surface of the northern edge of the arable field is strewn with rubble over an area of *c.* 100 × 50m. The rubble consists mainly of mortared flints, with a sprinkling of limestone, medieval brick and floor tile fragments, and human bones. Paul Drury has examined the floor tiles which include two groups, one relief decorated, the other slip decorated, of the late 13th to late 14th centuries. There is also one fragment of a plain Flemish 15th- or 16th-century tile, and one of a plain tile in an unusual fabric, probably a 14th-century import. Mr Drury comments 'The collection overall is most extraordinary for a small parish church, which in Norfolk usually yields little other than a few plain Flemish tiles.'

The excavation produced few finds that may have been derived from the church. Ten small fragments of limestone, two of clunch, and a few scraps of mortar were found in medieval and unstratified contexts.

Some years before 1980, a fragment of a late medieval terracotta panel was found by Mr Bert Reeve of East Harling close to the edge of Church Clump 'a few yards' west of the south-west corner of the excavation. A note by Paul Drury is on p.84.

IV. The Discovery of the Scattered Beonna Hoard and the Circumstances of the Excavation
(Figs 6 and 9)

In November 1980 Tony Frost, using a metal detector, found eight coins of Beonna on the ploughed surface of the field north of Church Clump in which Alan Davison had recovered Middle and Late Saxon material earlier that year, over an area measuring *c.* 10 × 5m (Fig. 4). The exact position of each find was carefully plotted by Mr Frost who immediately informed the Archaeology Department

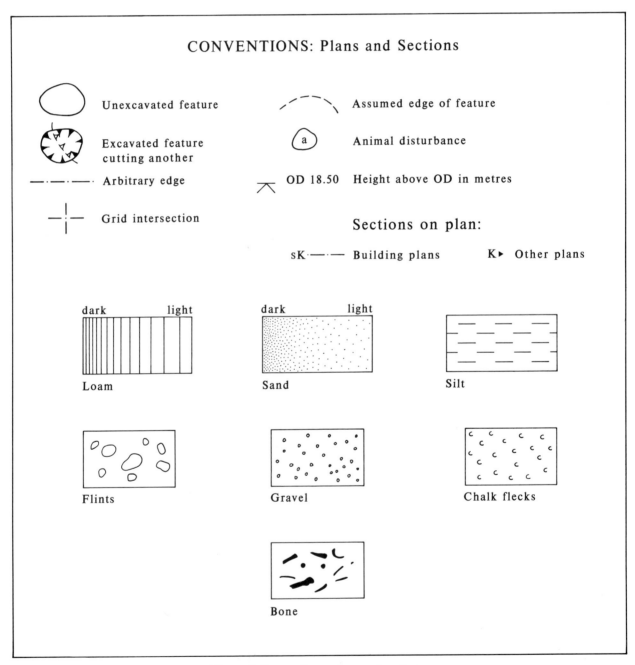

Figure 5 Conventions: plans and sections.

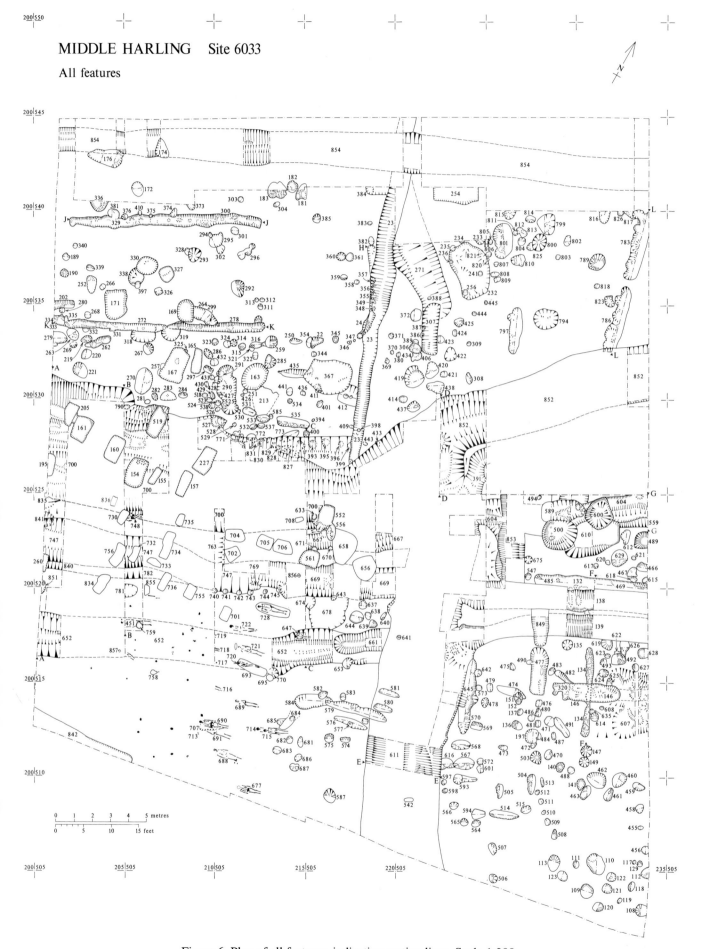

Figure 6 Plan of all features, indicating section lines. Scale 1:200.

7

Plate I Topsoil stripping and metal detecting in the south-west part of the excavation.

at Norwich Castle Museum (Fig. 9). As Mr Frost intended to continue his search, and because of disturbances to the ground surface by illicit metal detector users (who, in fact, had misjudged the location of the finds and had dug holes further to the east) the Norfolk Archaeological Unit decided to conduct a small-scale excavation with Tony Frost in order to locate any further coins. The work was carried out by the writer and Tony Frost, assisted by his father Mr Henry Frost, over ten days in late February and early March 1981. The excavation, which reached the surface of the natural sand over an area of *c.* 50m^2, produced another twenty-eight Beonna coins and a sceat along with pottery and metalwork of Middle and Late Saxon and medieval date. Post-holes, a ditch *(23)* and a pit *(367)* were partly excavated, but all the coins were recovered from the topsoil and from a layer of brown soil, which contained no evidence of features, and which lay below the topsoil and above the natural sand. This 'brown soil' appeared to be the result partly of earlier deeper ploughing and partly of root and perhaps animal disturbance of the surface of the natural subsoil and of archaeological features cut into it. The context of the coins, therefore, remained uncertain. The scattered hoard, along with another Beonna found by Mr Frost *c.* 100m to the south-south-west in 1980 (s.f. 58, Fig. 33; coin No. 67, p.48), were declared Treasure Trove at an Inquest in Diss in January 1982.

The British Museum, wishing to learn more about the circumstances of the hoard's deposition, undertook to finance an area excavation around the site of the 1981 trench. Work supervised by the writer began in October 1982 and continued for ten weeks. With the stripped area incompletely excavated, the British Museum sponsored a further nine week season in April–June 1983.

V. Methods of Excavation

The area of excavation was determined by the track to the north and by Church Clump to the south. The east and west edges were placed approximately equidistant from the site of the hoard.

The 1981 trench had shown that the ploughsoil was 25–30cm thick, and underlying brown soil was up to *c.* 40cm thick. It had also shown that metal artefacts, including Beonna coins, occurred in both layers of soil. It was felt that the mechanical removal of the topsoil in one spit would have involved the loss of coins (if further examples existed) because the metal detector could not operate through such a depth. As a result the topsoil was stripped in three spits of roughly equal depth. Metal detecting was carried out after each spit was removed (Plate I) and the co-ordinates of metal finds judged worthy of individual recording were plotted. The locations of these topsoil finds in the vertical plane were not recorded. After machining, the surface of the excavation (*i.e.* the upper surface of the brown soil) was cleaned by hoeing and trowelling and the resultant soil marks planned. These consisted of several amorphous patches, concentrations of human bones and two sets of sub-soiler scars, one parallel to the northern edge of Church Clump, and the other aligned with the track to the north. An initial attempt individually to excavate these scars was abandoned because of the length of time required, and thereafter the brown soil was shovelled off in spits averaging 10cm in depth. At first the areas covered by these spits were somewhat arbitrary but later they were excavated in blocks of 25m^2. Within spits the significant metal finds were recorded in three dimensions as 'small finds', while other finds were collected by spit and area and allocated context numbers. With the exception of some of the 18th-century

Plate II General view of excavation from the north, at end of 1983 season.

or later 'bone pits', the disturbed remains of a Late Saxon hearth *(213)*, and a few post-holes, particularly in the north-west part of the site, no archaeological features were visible on the cleaned surface of the brown soil. The excavated surface was regularly cleaned by hoeing during the removal in spits of the brown soil, but few clearly defined edges of cut features were recorded. Vertical soil changes were scarcely visible either, although once features cut into the natural were excavated and the brown soil, where it survived, was seen in section, then some stratification was recorded (for example in Sections AA–CC, Fig. 19). For the most part this consisted of the upper fillings of large ditches.

During the excavation of features, both large and small, care was taken to search their fillings with a metal detector before their removal. In most cases the detected objects were then found in normal manual excavation. Some small objects, however, were missed and were then detected after the bucket or barrow had been emptied on predetermined areas of the spoil heap. Only one artefact from the spoil heap (Fig. 47, No. 106) could not be provenanced. The use of the metal detector during the emptying of features was particularly effective in the case of those large features which were dug with hoes and shovels.

At the conclusion of the 1983 season the area of excavation had not been completely cleared down to the natural subsoil (Plate II). A strip along the northern edge, which included an east-to-west post-medieval ditch was left unexamined apart from several transverse trenches. Excavation did not reach the level of the natural subsoil over a rectangular area at 225–229/525–530 (Fig. 6). Work

was sufficient to trace the edges of the complex of east-to-west ditches in the central part of the site (Fig. 10), but large stretches of ditch were left unemptied. Only the upper surface of the graveyard in the south-west part of the excavated area was examined, so that we are left without any useful information on the density and chronology of burials.

During the 1982 season illicit metal detecting was carried out on the excavation at weekends. At the end of the season it was realised that with the site due to be left open until the following spring there was a real danger of damage to the excavation in the ensuing months. The decision was therefore taken, somewhat reluctantly, to remove all detectable metal objects. The sixty-one finds thus recovered were recorded three-dimensionally. Almost all were found in areas of brown soil above the natural subsoil, but they did include grave-goods from the western part of burial *451* (Fig. 22).

The use of a metal detector during all phases of the work was necessitated by the aims of the project: the complete recovery of the scattered Beonna hoard and the setting of the hoard in context. There is no doubt that the 'blanket' metal detecting of all contexts from the topsoil downwards slowed down and complicated excavation procedures, although it did not hinder the recovery of other forms of evidence. In the event, the frequency of metal artefacts in features was low, 18% of the total compared with 25.5% in the topsoil and 56.5% in brown soil. The reader must decide whether the exercise should be repeated and whether the results of the project have justified the methods used.

Chapter 2. Description of Excavation

I. Prehistoric Occupation
(Figs 7 and 8)

Artefactual evidence for prehistoric occupation is fully described and discussed below by Frances Healy. This evidence points to a predominantly Late Neolithic date for the occupation which was primarily associated with flint knapping. Apart from over 4000 pieces of struck flint and sixteen sherds of prehistoric pottery recovered from post-prehistoric contexts, three groups of Late Neolithic cut features were excavated.

In the north-west part of the site a group of four features produced Fengate ware and struck flints.

318: flat-based feature, max. depth 18cm, filled with pale brown silty sand.

319: scoop, max. depth 13cm; filled with brown sand.

327 (Fig. 8): small flat-based pit, max. depth 25cm, main filling of very dark brown sand. The northern half of the filling was dry-sieved (*342*).

338: small flat-based pit, max. depth 20cm, filled with dark brown loamy sand with profuse flints.

Two features (*794* and *823*) in the north-east part of the excavation produced Grooved Ware and flints including knapping debris, and another (*789*) contained a similar group of flints. All three contained later potsherds near their upper surfaces. The sandy natural in this area had been badly disturbed by ?roots.

789 (Fig. 8): small pit of cone-shaped profile, depth 55cm. Uppermost filling of dark brown sand (*784*), containing one sherd of Late Saxon pottery; middle filling of darker sand (*787*) and lower filling of yellowish brown sand (*788*).

794 (Plate III; Fig. 8): pit with undercut edges, depth 65cm. Upper filling of brown sand (*795*) producing one minute post-prehistoric sherd on the surface above black ashy sand (*796*).

823: very small pit, max. depth 20cm, filling of very dark greyish brown sand containing two small sherds of Late Saxon pottery near upper surface.

One feature (*674*) in the southern central area of the site produced Grooved Ware and cut another feature which contained no finds (*678*).

674: (Sect. CC, Fig. 19): feature of uncertain form, min. depth 8cm, filled with brown silty sand.

678: scoop, max. depth 10cm, filled with yellowish brown fine gravelly sand.

Evidence for later prehistoric activity in and near the excavated site was extremely limited. A late Bronze Age awl was recovered from a post-medieval context (Fig. 52 No. 134), and a contemporary forgery of an Iron Age stater was found on the surface *c.* 170m south-west of the excavation (coin No. 70, p.48).

II. The Roman Period

No evidence of Romano-British occupation was recovered. Sixty-three sherds of pottery and twenty fragments of tile were found in a wide variety of contexts. The pottery is predominantly late 1st- and 2nd-century greyware, and is probably derived from an occupation site, represented by a surface concentration of pottery of similar date lying *c.* 150m south-west of the excavation. It is uncertain whether the material arrived on the site as a result of manuring in the Roman period or of importation by later inhabitants of the excavated site. The former explanation is more likely in view of the small and abraded condition of most of the sherds.

Plate III Section of prehistoric pit *794* from the west.

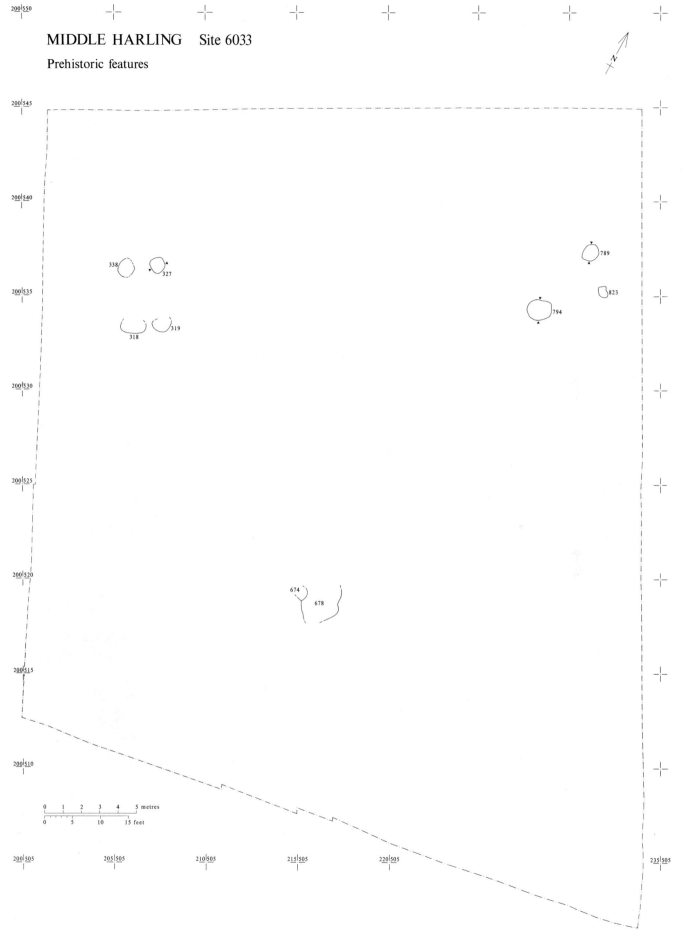

MIDDLE HARLING   Site 6033

Prehistoric features

Figure 7 Plan of prehistoric features. Scale 1:200.

11

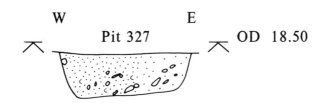

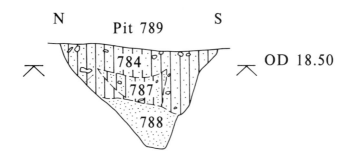

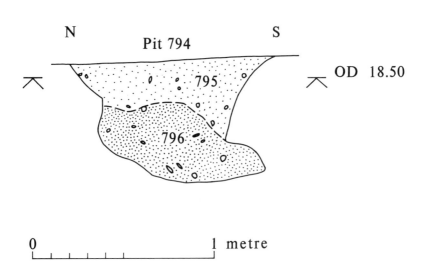

Figure 8 Sections of prehistoric pits *327, 789* and *794*. Scale 1:20.

Six Roman coins of the 1st to 4th centuries (coins Nos 72 and 74–8) were found on the site, including two recovered before the excavation and not listed by Marion Archibald (1985, 17). Of those described three had been mutilated, suggesting that they might have been deposited in post-Roman times. A pierced dupondius of Antoninus Pius was found south-west of the site (coin No. 73; Archibald 1985, 17, no. 2) and a sestertius of Domitian (coin No. 71) to the south.

III. The Early Saxon Period

There were no features of Early Saxon date, but a buckle was recovered from a post-medieval context (Fig. 40, No. 52). Part of an Early Saxon small-long brooch was found *c.* 160m west- south-west of the excavation site at TL 9785 8509 (Fig. 34, No. 1).

IV. The Middle Saxon Period
(Fig. 9)

In the absence of a stratified sequence, no excavated context could with any confidence be ascribed to the Middle Saxon period, despite the presence of the Beonna hoard, the sceattas, the other metal objects and the spread of potsherds. No Beonna coins were found in Middle Saxon features, and only one was recovered from a closed context. Coin No. 50 (Plate IV) was recovered from a small pit (*800*) which produced Late Saxon sherds, while a sceat (coin No. 1) was found in the upper filling of the possibly Middle Saxon ditch *661*. Some features containing no Late Saxon or later pottery may have been of Middle Saxon date. A substantial east-to-west ditch (*652*) (Figs 6 and 10; Sects. AA–CC, Fig. 19) contained only one Roman sherd and no disarticulated human bone, but was cut by a number of burials, including one of

MIDDLE HARLING
Middle Saxon finds

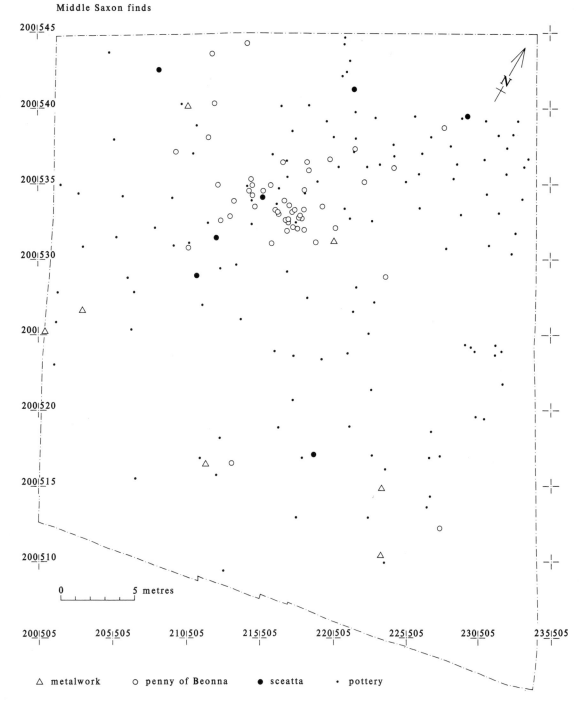

Figure 9 Plan of distribution of Middle Saxon coins, metalwork and pottery within area of excavation.
Scale 1:2500.

definite Late Saxon date. It was certainly filled before the establishment of the cemetery and might have been dug in the Middle Saxon period or earlier. Isolated post-holes containing Ipswich ware, but with no stratigraphical relationship with any deposit apart from the natural subsoil, were not certainly Middle Saxon. If one formed part of a structure which had been dated by other means to the Late Saxon period, as did post-hole *306* in Building B (it produced one sherd of Ipswich ware) then the sherd in question was clearly residual.

The distribution of Middle Saxon pottery in the excavated area (Fig. 9) shows that the greatest concentration of finds from the brown soil was in the north-eastern part, while the numbers of finds from features were roughly equal from all except the south-western quadrant. The latter, however, was incompletely excavated. Thirty-three sherds were recovered from features and ninety-seven from the brown soil, with five from the topsoil. Of the thirty-three only six sherds were found in features which did not contain later material and

Plate IV Beonna coin as found in pit *800* (coin no. 50).

were not associated with later buildings. The six sherds were recovered from six contexts: slot *202*, post-holes *349*, *445* and *593*, grave filling *723*, and small pit with human bones *758*. These were evenly spread across the excavated area in a pattern not dissimilar to that of the large number of features which produced no datable finds. Several ditches may have been dug in the Middle Saxon period, but stratigraphically all are merely pre-medieval. Ditch *652* (see above) may have formed a right-angle with the eastern and earliest phase of ditch *611*. The area thus enclosed could have contained an early phase of the cemetery. East-to-west ditch *139/661* may have been dug in the Middle Saxon times, but was undoubtedly much later than ditch *652*, being cut through the latter's upper filling. Ditch *559*, which was almost entirely removed by ditch *604*, was pre-medieval, but otherwise undatable. Ditch *782/840* was of similarly uncertain age.

With such flimsy evidence for Middle Saxon activity within the excavation, a possible first phase of the cemetery, some ditches which could well pre-date the period, a coin hoard, and a scatter of potsherds and other finds, it is very likely that the excavated area lies to the north of the Middle Saxon settlement site, the main focus of which was to the south of Church Clump as indicated by the large assemblage of pottery and metal finds from that area.

Ditch *139/661*
(Plate VI; Sect. FF, Fig. 19)
Entering the area of excavation from the east, this ditch terminated within the completely silted up and undated ditch *652*. It was stratigraphically earlier than ditch *138* and building D, and was cut by ditch *611*. One prehistoric sherd was found in the lowest filling (layer *127*, Sect. F–F) and medieval sherds in the uppermost filling (along with a sceat, coin No. 1, p.46). The lower layers within this ditch were markedly paler in colour and less humic than most other ditch fillings. It was certainly dug in pre-medieval times, and perhaps in the Saxon period. If Late Saxon, the lower fillings would probably have produced some Thetford-type ware. A Middle Saxon date is most likely.

Ditch *559*
(Sect. GG, Fig. 20)
Aligned east-to-west this feature had been almost destroyed by ditch *604* and other medieval features. Its pale non-humic filling produced worked flints only; it may possibly have been dug in the Middle Saxon period.

Ditch *652*
(Plate V; Sects AA, BB, CC, Fig. 19)
Entering the western edge of the excavation ditch *652* terminated beneath the later north-to-south ditch *611*, although it may have turned through 90° and continued south as the eastern part of *611*. The fillings of *652* were in the main pale and low in humic content. Apart from worked flints and animal bones, the only find was a sherd of Romano-British greyware from the upper filling (layer *737*) immediately west of Section C–C. At least seven burials cut the upper filling, including accompanied burial *451* of Late Saxon date and one other (*720*) whose filling produced a Romano-British and a Middle Saxon sherd. Towards its eastern end *652* was cut by ditch *139/661* which was possibly Middle Saxon. The date of *652* itself remains uncertain, although if it had been filled in the Middle Saxon period some Ipswich ware might have been found within the considerable amount of filling excavated.

Ditch *782/840*
(Sects AA and BB, Fig. 19)
The eastern extent of this ditch had been completely removed by ditch *747*, while the western lay beyond the edge of the excavation. No finds apart from a few animal bones were made in the two sections cut across it. A pre-medieval date is most likely.

V. The Late Saxon and Saxo-Norman Periods
(Figs 6 and 10–12)

There was abundant evidence of Late Saxon and Saxo-Norman occupation, in the form of both finds and features, within the northern half and south-eastern part of the excavated site. The earliest and most northern cuts of ditch complex *700* along with ditch *23* enclosed an area containing Building A, while ditch *23* was cut through Building B. South and east of Building A three shallow pits (*270*, *290*, *367*) contained Late Saxon finds, and one of these (*290*) cut the west wall of Building B. Another pit (*330*) lay near the centre of Building A.

Ditch *23* was later than ditch *271* which was also cut by slot *307*. The latter formed part of the west wall of Building E, a somewhat dubious structure which was aligned north-to-south and which, from the evidence of one sherd of early medieval ware, may date to the 11th century. In the extreme north-east corner of the site two features (*783* and *786*) formed the west wall of post-in-trench Building C, the majority of which lay outside the excavation. This structure was aligned parallel to ditch *23*, and again, from pottery evidence, may have been 11th-century.

Apart from the northern part of ditch complex *700* none of the great swathe of ditches in the central part of the site were of Late Saxon date (see p.24). Despite the presence of large quantities of Late Saxon finds in the south-eastern part of the site, no certainly Late Saxon features were recorded, although two post-holes (*141* and *151*), a short length of slot cut by medieval Building D

14

Plate V Section of ditch *652* from the east.

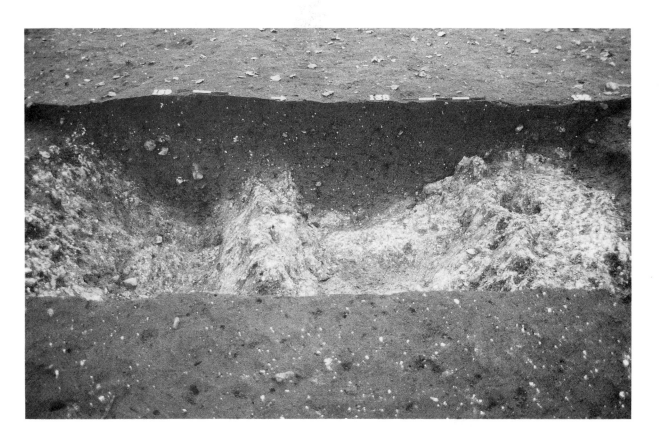

Plate VI Section of ditches *138* and *139* from the east.

15

MIDDLE HARLING   Site 6033

The ditches

Figure 10 Plan: ditches of all periods. Scale 1:200.

16

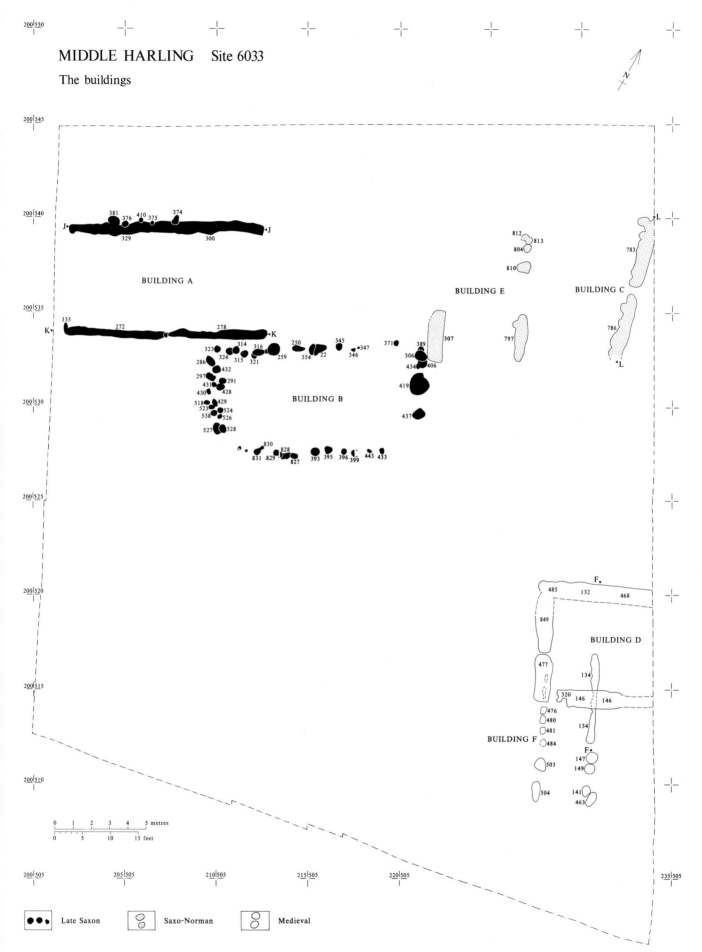

Figure 11 Plan: Late Saxon, Saxo-Norman and medieval buildings. Scale 1:200.

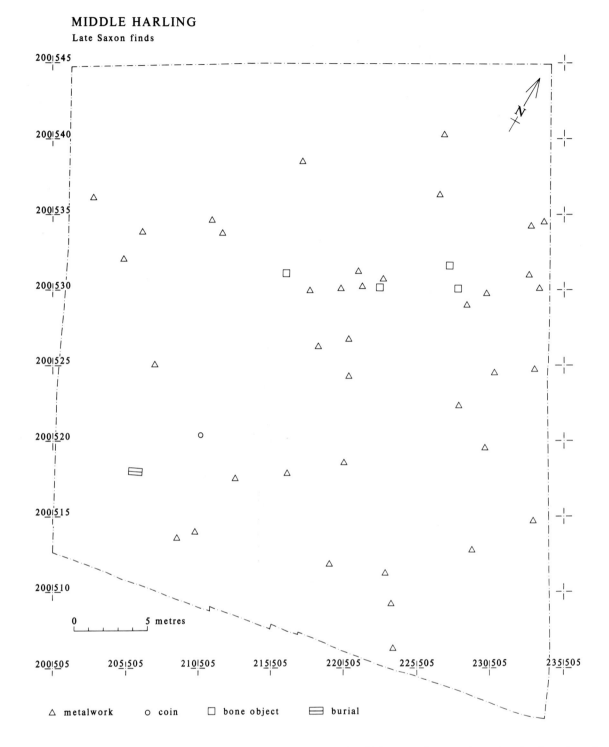

Figure 12 Plan of distribution of Late Saxon coins and metalwork within area of excavation, showing location of burial *451*. Scale 1:250.

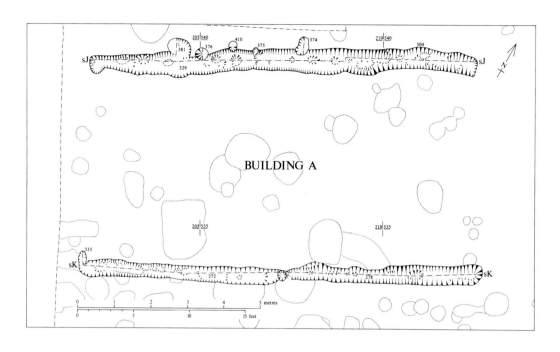

Figure 13 Plan: Building A. Scale 1:100.

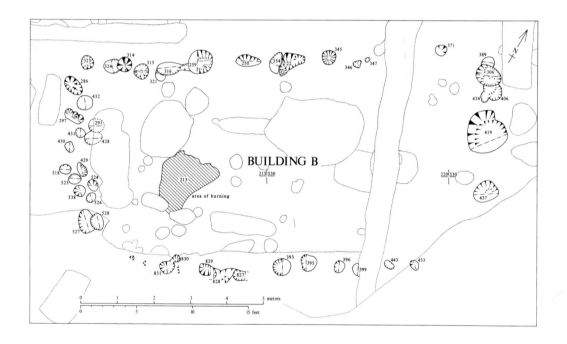

Figure 14 Plan: Building B. Scale 1:100.

19

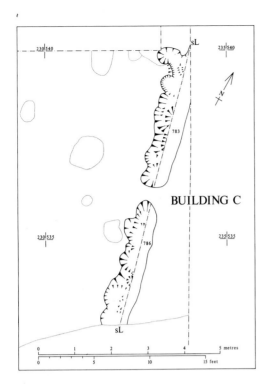

Figure 15 Plan: Building C. Scale 1:100.

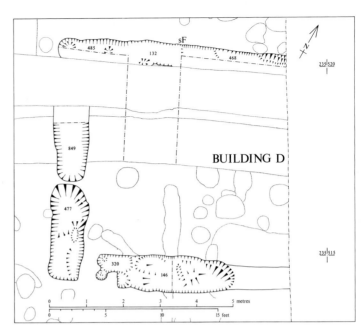

Figure 16 Plan: Building D. Scale 1:100.

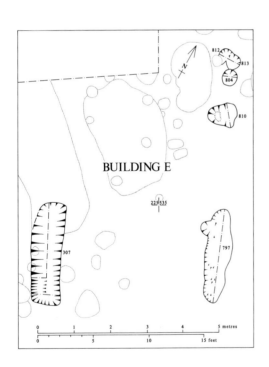

Figure 17 Plan: Building E. Scale 1:100.

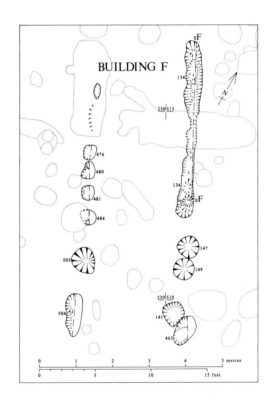

Figure 18 Plan: Building F. Scale 1:100.

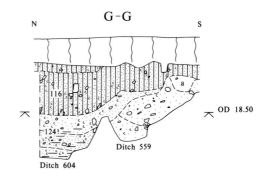

G-G

N   S

116

a

OD 18.50

124

Ditch 559

Ditch 604

W

329

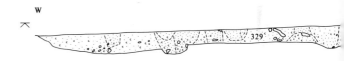

W

272

0   1   2 metres

NE

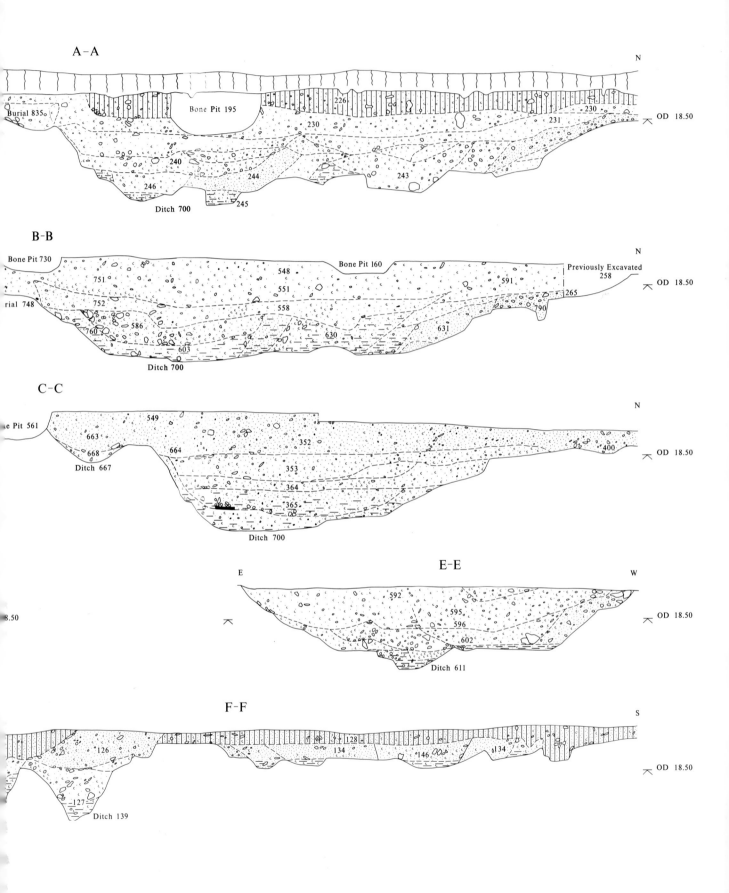

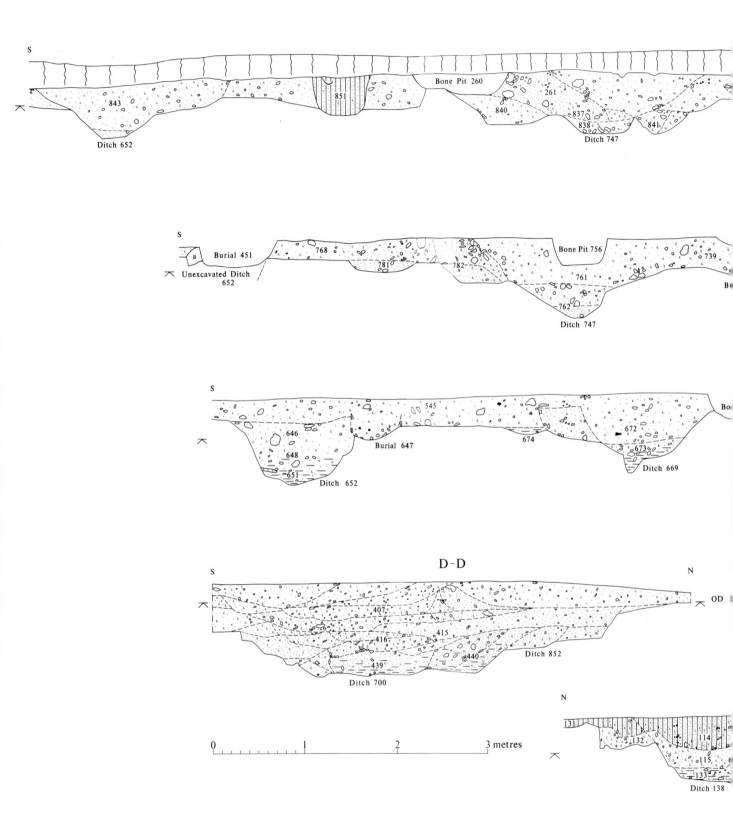

Figure 19 Sections A–A to F–F. Scale 1:40.

21

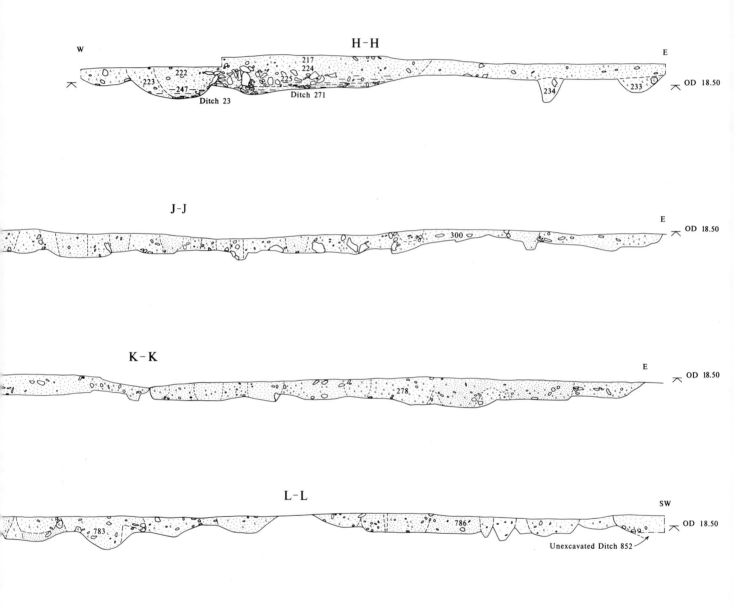

Figure 20 Sections G–G to L–L. Scale 1:40.

Plate VII Building A from the west.

(*482*) and a small pit (*629*) all contained pottery of this date without later material.

It is certain that at least one burial in the cemetery belongs to this period. Burial *451* which was accompanied by grave-goods is described below. Some other burials may have been Late Saxon for it is difficult to see burial *451* as an isolated singleton, while three or four were medieval. However, it is likely that burials to the north of the church would not have been numerous in either period.

By the 10th century the excavated area lay within a settlement that had outgrown its Middle Saxon predecessor. Not only had the densely settled area grown north from the church as far as the east-to-west track, but on the evidence of surface finds it had also expanded to the west and more especially to the east, of Church Clump. There was also some expansion southwards. The main component of the Late Saxon occupation was certainly domestic, there being little evidence for industrial activity. Building B contained the remnants of a hearth, but there was no signs of one in Building A, which may have been floored at a higher and more disturbed level.

Building A
(Plate VII; Fig. 13, Sects JJ and KK, Fig. 20)
The evidence for this structure consisted of two parallel east-to-west slots cut into the natural subsoil. These slots (*329/300* and *272/278*) showed no sign of post-settings in the upper surface of their fillings, despite repeated cleaning, but in longitudinal section there were possible indications of posts in *329* and *278*. The soil-marks were accompanied in some cases by minor deepenings in the bases of the slots. The shape and size of posts remain uncertain. Slot *329/300* was continuous while *272* and *278* had been dug out separately, there being a marked narrowing of their widths where they touched in the approximate centre of the south wall. No traces of end

walls were noted although a probable post-hole (*335*) was situated at the western end of the southern wall (*272*). Both features were apparently filled at the same time. Other post-holes at each end, *e.g. 311–13, 189–90* may possibly relate to the structure. A series of post-holes (*381, 376, 410, 375* and *374*) cut the northern edge of the northern slot (*329*) and may have been inserted during a rebuilding phase. There was no evidence of flooring or of a hearth. The structure measured *c.* 10.3 × 6.1m externally.

Only two potsherds (Thetford-type ware) were found in clear association with the structure, in the fillings of slots *272* and *300*. Large amounts of Thetford-type ware from spits in the general area of the building suggest a Late Saxon date for its use, while an 8th/9th century decorated copper alloy pin-head (Fig. 36, No. 21) was found 8cm above the surface of the natural within the interior at co-ordinate 210.90/534.70.

Building B
(Figs 14 and 21)
The forty-six post-holes that comprise the evidence for this structure were excavated in each of the three seasons of work, and were not recognised as a possible building until after digging had finished. As a consequence half-sections were aligned at many different angles. In addition features became apparent at differing depths because of the frequent and confusing changes in the subsoil from discoloured sand to degraded chalk. These factors have led to the presentation of stylised block sections (Fig. 21) which show the recorded upper surface and base of each post-hole, rather than conventional sections.

Post-holes were of varying depths and diameters and few showed clear indications of posts. Post-hole *259* in the north wall contained a central vertical feature loosely filled with dark soil, rectangular in plan, and measuring

10cm north-to-south and min. 40cm east-to-west. This feature may have been caused by the rotting of a vertically-set plank. Post-hole *419* in the east wall took the form of a shallow scoop containing a roughly circular central dark filling, diam. *c.* 30cm, and there was a probable post-impression at the base of post-hole *437*. The structure measured *c.* 12 × 6m externally.

A number of post-holes along all wall-lines were intercutting. This indicates a phase or phases of rebuilding. The jumble of post-holes forming the west wall could be simplified by ignoring all except a roughly straight row which includes, from north-to-south, *323, 432, 431, 429, 538* and *527*.

An irregularly shaped area of burnt clay flecks with some fire-cracked flints (*213*) was situated towards the west end of the structure. It was visible at the base of the brown soil and overlay a thin layer of soil above the natural subsoil. It had no definite relationship with any post-holes, and there was no trace of a surrounding floor. It was probably the remains of a hearth.

Late Saxon ditch *23* cut post-hole *399* in the south wall and removed part of the north wall, while most of the south wall was truncated by the northern edge of ditch complex *700*. Features within the building were datable except for pits *367* and *290*, and a short length of slot *435* which contained Thetford-type ware. Pit *290* cut post-holes *291* and *428* in the west wall. Post-holes produced twelve potsherds including one unidentified, one Ipswich ware, one Tating ware, seven Thetford-type ware and two St Neots-type ware. Although none of these sherds could be definitely associated with either the construction or the demolition of the building, because the excavation did not differentiate between post packing, post sockets and post withdrawal, it is likely that the structure was erected and used in the Late Saxon period.

Building C
(Fig. 15; Sect. LL, Fig. 19)
One wall of a structure was represented by two slots, *783* and *786*, the remainder of the evidence lying outside the excavation. No sign of posts was visible on the cleaned surface of the filling, and the longitudinal section was similarly uninformative. However, the shape of the features in plan and profile as well as their fillings indicated that they were not ditches. The southern extent of *786* was cut away by medieval ditch *852*. The alignment of the slots was roughly parallel with Late Saxon ditch *23* which lay *c.* 12m to the west. Pottery from the slots comprised two sherds of Early Medieval ware, two of Thetford-type and one of St Neots ware.

Building E
(Fig. 17)
This problematic structure consisted of two short slots (*307* and *797*) aligned north-to-south, the former cutting the southern end of Late Saxon ditch *271*. Four post-holes (*804, 810, 812* and *813*) might have continued the eastern wall line. Equivalent post-holes to the north of *307* may have gone unrecorded in the filling of ditch *271* and outside the completely excavated area. There was no relationship between slot *307* and post-hole *306* in the east wall of Building B. Features *307* and *797* produced eight Late Saxon sherds and one of Early Medieval ware.

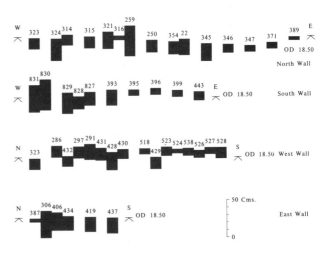

Figure 21 Schematic sections of post-holes in Building B. Vertical scale 1:50.

Ditch *23*
(Sect. HH, Fig. 20)
The southern part of this ditch had a uniform filling while the northern part had been recut on one occasion. It cut ditch *271*, Building B, and a series of post-holes and slots to the north of Building B, and was cut by medieval ditch *700* and post-medieval ditch *854*. One sherd of Early Medieval pottery was recovered from the central stretch, but a total of seventeen Late Saxon sherds was found in the fillings. It was first dug after the life of Late Saxon Building B, and was being filled in the 11th century. Ditch *23* was aligned at 90° to the earlier phases of ditch *700*.

Ditch *271*
(Sect. HH, Fig. 20)
The southern terminal of a shallow ditch-like feature was cut by ditch *23*. Above some basal silting the filling was unusual for the quantity of flint boulders and gravel. Only five sherds of Late Saxon pottery were recovered. The southern end was cut by slot *307* (Building E).

Ditch *391*
A curving fragment of this apparent ditch was recorded only in one small part of the site (at co-ordinate 224.50/526), where a multiplicity of ditches coincided with incomplete excavation. It was earlier than ditch *700*, and other nearby ditches, and was probably a continuation of a ditch along the line later taken by ditch *611*. It may have been of Late Saxon date.

Ditch *700*
(Plate VIII; Sect. AA and BB, Fig. 19)
The northern part of this ditch complex in its western half contained Late Saxon sherds in the upper fillings. The ditch has been recut progressively from north to south, and it seems likely that the earlier phases were cut in the Late Saxon period (Fig. 10). This is described more fully on p.26.

Burial *451*
(Fig. 22)
This burial, which cut ditch *652*, was partly excavated at the end of the 1982 season when the unexcavated parts of the site were cleared of detectable metal objects. Excavation was completed in 1983. The bones, which were in poor condition, were submitted to Rosemary

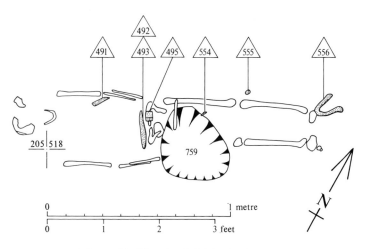

Figure 22 Plan: Burial *451*. Scale 1:20.

Powers for examination. Unfortunately the cranial fragments were mislaid on the London Underground before arrival at the British Museum (Natural History). The surviving bones suggest a possible male burial (p.84). Grave goods indicate this is a burial of the late 9th or early 10th century. Thus it can join the very small number of accompanied inhumations of this date known in East Anglia, and can confidently be identified as the burial of a pagan Viking.

A knife (s.f. 491, Fig. 76, No. 7) lay immediately within the left elbow. A copper alloy buckle with iron plate (s.f. 495, Fig. 76, No. 1) was found on the left pelvis. Directly to the west a honestone (s.f. 493, Fig. 76, No. 8) was overlain by a knife (s.f. 492, Fig. 76, No. 6) which was covered by a pivoting bladed knife (s.f. 492, Fig. 76, No. 4). Both knives were placed with tips to the north and cutting edges to the west. On the west edge of the honestone another pivoting bladed knife (s.f. 492, Fig. 76, No. 5) was set cutting edge upwards with tip also facing north. A small iron buckle was placed just to the north-east of the left knee (s.f. 555, Fig. 76, No. 2). A spur (s.f. 556, Fig. 76, No. 9) lay next to the left foot. A copper alloy nail cleaner (s.f. 554, Fig. 76, No. 3) was found in the filling 11cm above the base of the grave. A post-hole (*759*) had destroyed the area of the right thigh. The grave filling produced one sherd of Thetford-type ware.

VI. The Medieval Period
(Figs 6, 10 and 11)

It is very likely that there was continuity on the excavated site from the 11th into the 13th century, with occupation moving away by *c.* 1250. A settlement site, evidenced by surface finds of pottery, metalwork and coins, and situated to the north of the excavation at TL 9797 8525, continued into the 16th century. East of the excavation and south of Church Clump there is no surface evidence of occupation beyond *c.* 1250. This lack of later medieval activity around the church may have been the result of settlement movement or of decline. The latter seems more likely in view of the evidence of the 1334 Lay Subsidy (p.2).

Within the excavated area the most striking element was the array of ditches that traversed the site from east to west (Fig. 10). Excavation failed to unravel this complex,

and was insufficient in extent to trace the course of the ditches to east and west. With their extent and layout unknown, their function remains equally obscure. Ditches *700* and *747* probably served as shifting northern graveyard boundaries, as did ditch *611* to the east. However, the need to redefine the northern limits of the graveyard so often and with such deep ditch cuts is difficult to explain. Equally curious is the coincidence of the change in alignment between ditch *700* and *852* with the southern end of Late Saxon north-to-south ditch *23*.

No medieval features occurred north of ditches *700* and *852*. At least three burials were medieval. Occupation in the south-east corner of the site was fairly intense. A narrow building (F) aligned north-to-south was replaced by a larger structure (D) set at 90° to it. The latter was cut through by ditch *138*. North of Building D a cluster of pits (*500, 589, 600* and *610*), probably dug as receptacles for cess and/or rubbish, was probably in use throughout the life of both buildings. An area north of these pits was left unexcavated, but it is likely that ditch *852* in some way marked the boundary of the medieval occupation.

It would be unwise to conjecture upon the status of the medieval occupation of the excavated site and its immediate surroundings, because of the restricted area examined. Whether a fragment of a peasant holding, a Rectory, or a manorial complex has been glimpsed, it cannot now be said. However, the presence on site on at least one occasion during the early 13th century of Jeffrey de Furneaux, Lord of Middle Harling, can be assumed from his silver seal matrix (Fig. 44, No. 81) found in topsoil over ditch *611*.

Building D
(Fig.16; Sect. FF, Fig. 19)
The north, south and west walls of a structure were represented by slots *485/132/468, 146* and *477/849*. The eastern extent of the building lay outside the excavation. The broad and relatively flat-based slots produced no evidence of post-settings in their uniform fillings, although circular depressions in the base were recorded in *132/485* and *146*. The eastern end of *146* appeared to be rounded. East of this terminal the surface of the natural was badly disturbed by probable tree holes and no definite continuation of *146* was detectable. However, in section

25

in the east edge of the excavation, a flat-based feature was faintly visible in a location that suggested it was associated with *146*. Slot *849*, cut the surface of ditch *139*, the upper filling of which was medieval. The north wall (*485/132/468*) was cut by medieval ditch *138*. The south wall (*146*) cut slot *134*, part of the east wall of medieval Building F. Slot fillings produced fifteen sherds of medieval pottery as well as earlier material.

Building F
(Fig.18; Sect. FF, Fig. 19)
Evidence for this building consisted of alignments of post-holes and a slot. The west wall was carried on six post-holes (*476, 480, 481, 484, 503* and *504*) and the northern part of the wall was represented by two (unnumbered) deepenings in the base of slot *477*. The east wall comprised a slot (*134*) to the north of three post-holes (*147, 149* and *141*). At the southern end of this wall post-hole *463* may indicate an extension, as may the southern shallower part of *504* in the west wall. There was no evidence for north and south walls. The structure measured *c*. 7.5–8 × 3m externally. Both wall lines were cut by slots (*146* and *477*) of medieval Building D. Slot and post-hole fillings produced eight sherds of medieval pottery.

Ditch 138/669/747
(Plate VI; Sects AA, BB, CC, FF, Fig. 19)
This ditch traversed the site from east-to-west. It cut the undated but 'early' ditch *782*, and was later than ditch *139*. Its relationships with ditches *611* and *853* were uncertain. Between stretches *747* and *669* there was a marked narrowing of width, but there was no indication of recutting in the filling. An alignment of post-holes (*74–3*) cut the southern edge of *747*, but another to the east in the same line was cut by *669*. The cut of the latter was therefore later. Medieval pottery was recovered from the primary silts of all three stretches. Disarticulated human bones were found in all sections through *747* but did not occur in the filling of *669*.

Ditch 604/667
(Sect. GG, Fig. 20)
Running east-to-west, ditch *604/667* had no discernible relationship with the northern end of ditch *611* but was cut by ditch *853*. To the west its course was not revealed by excavation but it certainly turned or terminated to east of easting 210. Pottery finds suggest that it was being filled in the medieval period.

Ditch 611
(Plate IX; Sect. EE, Fig. 19)
This consisted of a succession of north-to-south ditches with a termination to the north which was inadequately examined. An earlier phase to the east terminated further to the south in a position which suggests that it may have been related to the east-west ditch *652*. The later western ditch, which showed evidence of recutting, produced medieval pottery from the base of the recut (layer *602*) in the one complete cross-section excavated. The only datable finds from the earlier eastern phase, two sherds of Thetford-type ware, occurred in the uppermost filling (layer *592*), although five medieval sherds were found in similar filling (*754* and *774*) further to the north during

excavation of the eastern edge of the ditch. The western ditch cut ditches *139/661* and *652*.

Ditch 700
(Plate VIII; Sects AA, BB and CC, Fig. 19)
Three sections were cut across a major east-west soilmark which traversed the west-central part of the site. The western and middle sections (AA and BB) showed that there was a series of ditches progressively recut from north-to-south, but there were considerable difficulties in correlating the two records. A lack of longitudinal sections certainly hampered interpretation of the sequence. The plan of ditches (Fig. 10) attempts to indicate the most likely lines of the various recuts. No late medieval or later finds were recovered from the upper fillings and this suggests that by the 14th or 15th century there was probably little surface evidence of ditches. Dating of the sequence of recuts is uncertain because of the small quantities of datable finds recovered from each section. In the westernmost trench, layer *245* produced Thetford-type ware and layer *244* medieval, as did layer *240*. None of the deposits in the northern part of the trench below layer *230* contained datable finds. Medieval pottery was found in basal layer *603* (Sect. BB). Layer *630* was devoid of pottery, as was *631*. In the cutting containing Sect. CC where there was no evidence of recutting, layer *353* produced medieval pottery but there were no datable finds below this. At its eastern end ditch *700* was observed, in plan, to cut ditch *852*. In section D-D layer *439*, silting at the base of a recut contained medieval pottery, but layer *440* at the base of an earlier cut was devoid of datable finds.

Although excavation was insufficient to be certain in detail, it is clear that the southern recuts of ditch *700* were medieval, while the northern phases, containing Late Saxon sherds in their upper filling, were of earlier date. Their alignment, however, was at 90° to that of ditch *23* which was undoubtedly Late Saxon. They are therefore probably of the same date.

Ditch 852
(Sect. DD, Fig. 19)
Only the western end of this feature was excavated, although the northern edge was recorded as a soil mark and the upper filling was emptied against the eastern edge of the excavation. The western end was cut by the terminal of ditch complex *700*, and the northern edge cut slot *786* of Saxo-Norman Building C. The primary silting of *852* adjacent to ditch complex *700* produced one medieval sherd.

Ditch 853
The southern end of this north-to-south ditch had no discernible relationship with ditch *138*, and it cut medieval ditch *604*. Its northern extent was unrecorded in an incompletely excavated area of the site.

The Cemetery
(Fig. 23)
The area of the cemetery, which must have belonged to St Andrew's church to the south-west, was incompletely excavated, particularly in the western part. The area was bounded by ditch *700* to the north and ditch *611* to the east. With a few exceptions burials were not excavated and the natural subsoil was not exposed. However, it was clear that here there was little build-up of brown soil between the

Plate VIII Section of ditch *700* from the east, as north end of Section B–B.

Plate IX Section of ditch *611* from the north, as Section E–E.

27

The burials

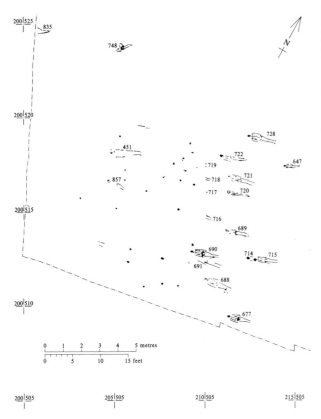

Figure 23 Plan: burials, south-west area of excavation.
Scale 1:200.

Plate X Burial *748*, with bone pit *730* in section above.

base of the ploughsoil and the natural, and excavation was sufficient to show that the part of the cemetery which impinged upon the excavation was far from densely packed. The plan (Fig. 23) shows all bones there were judged to be *in situ*. These include many skulls on their own with the remainder of the skeletons unexposed by excavation. Grave outlines were in almost all cases unclear in plan, although that around burial *728* was very definite. Where recorded, all burials were aligned with heads to the west. Only one (burial *451*) was accompanied by grave-goods and was Late Saxon. Apart from this there were few indications of date. Burial *690*, which cut another, *691*, overlay a grave-shaped feature (*707*) containing a medieval sherd. The two northernmost burials (*748* and *835*) were cut through soil containing medieval pottery into the southern edge of ditch *700* (Plate X). Seven burials (and probably many others) were cut into the upper filling of ditch *562*.

Apart from the post-medieval bone pits described below numerous other contexts produced human bones. All were west of easting *220* apart from two fragments from spit *775* (co-ordinate 225–30/535–40). Fragments were found in a post-medieval pit (*176*) near the north-west corner, and in most of the hand-excavated spits in the western half, with quantities increasing to the south. The filling of ditch *747* contained human bones (layers *837* and *761*, Sects AA and BB, Fig. 19; layer *746* at co-ordinate 210/520) as did layers over ditch complex *700* (layers *230* and *231*, Sect. AA, Fig. 19; layers *548, 551,*

558, 751 and *752*, Sect. BB, Fig. 19). Further bones were recovered from layers in the latest recuts of *700* (*246* and *586* in Sects AA and BB, Fig. 19).

From the above evidence it is clear that there had been considerable disturbance of burials long before the final destruction of the church in *c.* 1743.

VII. Post-Medieval and Recent
(Figs 6, 24 and 25)

The northern edge of the excavation was closely followed by an east to west ditch (*854*) of post-medieval date. This ran parallel to the track heading west towards West Harling, and its upper filling was cut by two amorphous pits (*174* and *176*).

In the south-west corner of the excavation a substantial flat-based and almost vertically-sided feature (*842*), 30cm deep, was probably the north-east edge of a chalk quarry, perhaps that which caused such outrage in the mid-18th century on the site of St Andrew's church (p.4–5). The filling contained a few human bones.

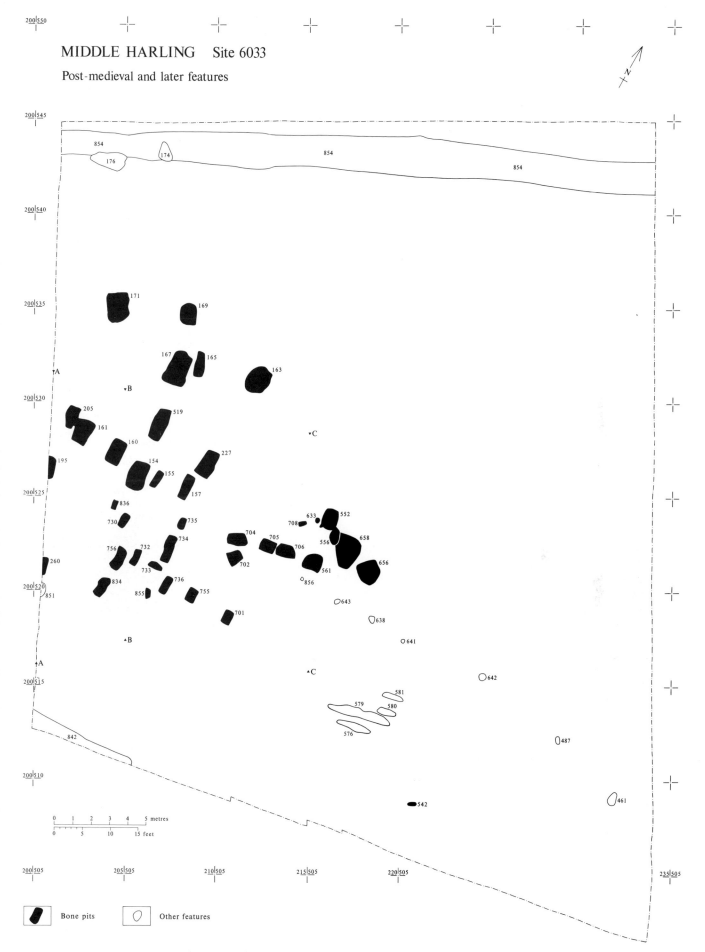

MIDDLE HARLING   Site 6033

Post-medieval and later features

Figure 24 Plan: post-medieval and modern features. Scale 1:200.

29

Plate XI Bone pits *154* and *155* before excavation, from the east.

Plate XII Bone pits *154* and *155* after cleaning, from the east.

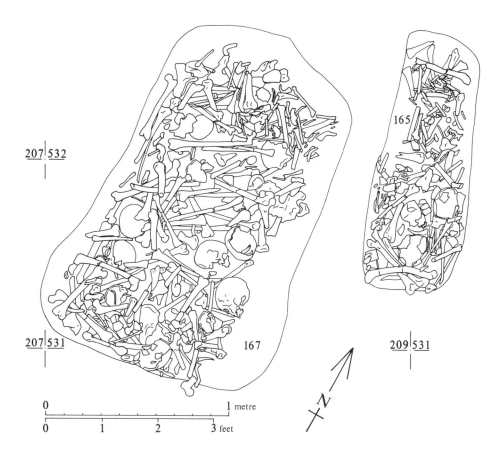

207|532

165

207|531

209|531

167

0   1 metre
0   1   2   3 feet

N

Figure 25 Plan: bone pits *165* and *167*. Scale 1:20.

Thirty-nine pits crammed with disarticulated human bones were recorded, predominantly in the north-west part of the site. Many were visible as concentrations of bone immediately below the ploughsoil, and all those encountered in the first season of excavation were meticulously recorded in plan and emptied of bones (Plates XI and XII). A plan of two adjacent pits (*165* and *167*) is published as an example (Fig. 25). In the second season only those which cut features in need of excavation were emptied, because it was then realised that the pits were of late date. Many of them were cut into the uppermost fillings of medieval ditches, and the filling of one pit (*702*) produced a post-medieval copper alloy button. The multiplicity of pits suggests a number of occasions of reburial, and as the church and graveyard were finally desecrated in *c.* 1743 the pits must post-date this time. The extraction of chalk from the area of the graveyard, presumably carried out for marling purposes, would have been done on a seasonal basis. It can only be assumed that the later 18th or 19th-century chalk diggers held human remains in higher regard than did those who had earlier removed the church foundations.

The contents of one pit (*167*) have been examined by Rosemary Powers (p.84–6). A minimum of forty-six individuals of varying ages and both sexes are represented.

Two small pits in the area of the cemetery which contained loosely packed redeposited human bones (*695* and *758*) are probably contemporary with the use of the cemetery, and the upper filling (*693*) above burial *720* contained a similar deposit of disturbed bones.

An alignment of seven post-holes (*461, 487, 638, 641–3* and *856*), most of which were filled with soil similar to the ploughsoil, and three of which retained remains of circular wooden posts, probably represents a former northern boundary of Church Clump. The boundary shown on the O.S. 1905 edition of the 1:2500 map was convex and further to the north than at present, but slightly to the south of these post-holes. No further examples were observed to the west of post-hole *856*, but the general alignment of the boundary continued through the area of bone pits as a division between predominantly larger pits to the north and smaller ones to the south.

Linear features *576* and *579–81* were also filled with topsoil and were parallel to plough and subsoiler marks recorded below the ploughsoil after machine stripping. They were probably the result of a localised and accidental deepening of mechanical cultivation.

Feature *851* (Sect, AA, Fig. 19) was filled with topsoil, containing human bone and a flower-pot sherd.

Ditch *854*

This ditch was on average 43cm deep and ran parallel to the east-west track which lay immediately to the north of the excavation. Although most finds were Late Saxon and medieval, post-medieval pottery and glass from the basal filling indicates that it was silting up in the 18th century, and was probably first dug out not much earlier.

Chapter 3. The Artefacts

I. Prehistoric Material
by Frances Healy

Written August 1984, revised October 1993

Note: Chronology is expressed in radiocarbon years BP and calibrated radiocarbon years BC. Calibrations of individual determinations are expressed at two sigma and are derived from the datasets of Pearson and Stuiver (1986) and Pearson *et al.* (1986), using the University of Washington Quaternary Isotope Laboratory Radiocarbon Calibration Program 1987 revision 2.0.

Lithic Material

Description

1. Distribution and presentation. The composition and incidence of lithic material are summarised in Table 1, with material from prehistoric contexts broken down by stratigraphic unit in Table 2 (microfiche). Selected pieces are illustrated in Figures 28–30 and described in Table 11. Figure 26 shows the density and distribution of lithic material from those non-prehistoric contexts which can be attributed to 5m squares. The resulting pattern is distorted, since differing volumes of deposit were excavated from each square. Despite this limitation, it is possible to see slight increases in density near prehistoric features rich in lithic material, in 5m squares 205 535, 225 530, and 230 530. The highest density, however, is in 5m square 215 515, coinciding with pits *674* and *678*, which contained no lithic material at all, although *674* yielded four sherds of Grooved Ware. The second highest, in 5m square 230 520, corresponds to no surviving prehistoric feature. Both concentrations may be partly attributable to the excavation of deep post-prehistoric ditches, but not wholly so, since comparable densities do not obtain in other squares, such as 215 525, 220 520, or 220 535, where deep ditches were also excavated.

Material from the north-east and north-west groups of pits is presented separately, as is that from the two largest concentrations, in an attempt to assess the relation of the contents of the groups of pits to each other and to the residual and unstratified material.

2. Raw material. S1, an axe fragment, has been identified by R. V. Davis as an uralitised gabbro of the type generally associated with petrological group I. This is traditionally attributed to an unlocated source near Penzance, Cornwall, although a source of similar rock has recently been discovered in the north-west of England (Davis 1985, 34). The flint of which the bulk of the artefacts is made was, however, almost certainly collected in the immediate neighbourhood. When the surrounding fields are bare of crops they are, like the rest of the Breckland, scattered with fragments, pebbles and nodules of flint, some of them large. This abundant local supply matches the excavated struck flint in colour (black to grey, sometimes thinly banded with pale grey or white, with thin white or cream cortex) and in condition (with weathered surfaces, and with both superficial and latent thermal fractures). There seems little doubt that it provided the raw material for most of the collection. An exception is a large flake from pit *823*, which is of sound, dark, fresh flint with up to 16mm of dense, cream cortex, and is visually comparable with Grime's Graves floorstone.

3. Condition. Flint from prehistoric features is fresh, sharp, and matt, with relatively little edge-damage. Flint from post-prehistoric contexts is generally abraded and glossy, probably sand-polished, since the region was formerly prone to sand-blows. The polish itself is often cut by more recent edge-damage. In these circumstances, the lightly-retouched edges of serrated pieces, which were well-preserved in the pits (*e.g.* F3, F18, F24), are likely to have been damaged beyond recognition in other contexts. This is almost certainly why this form amounts to only 13% of retouched pieces from non-prehistoric contexts in contrast to 25% of those from prehistoric contexts (Table 1). The flint from pits *789* and *823*, which contained small quantities of Late Saxon pottery, is in the same fresh condition as that from unequivocally prehistoric contexts and, like the material from pits *327*, *338*, and *794*, includes extremely small, sharp flakes which suggest that it was not transported far, if at all, from its original knapping site. For this reason, *789* and *823* are treated as prehistoric features.

4. Composition and typology. The overall composition of each group is set out in Table 3. Irregular waste consists largely of fragments like F12, which exhibit both thermal fractures and flake scars and which seem to have resulted from the attempted working of defective raw material. Core typology is summarised in Table 4, and the dimensions and proportions of selected groups of complete, unretouched flakes in Figure 27. Length was measured at the maximum dimension along the bulbar axis at right-angles to the striking platform and breadth at the maximum distance between any two points on opposite lateral edges taken at right-angles to the length measurement (Saville 1981a). For reasons of time and practicality, only flakes over 10mm long were measured, although many smaller flakes were present, especially in pit *794*. 'Primary', 'secondary' and 'tertiary' are used to denote flakes the dorsal faces of which are respectively completely cortical, partly cortical and non-cortical. Since pits *318*, *319*, *327*, and *338* were almost certainly contemporary, the flakes from them were added together. Since less certainty attaches to the contemporaneity of pits *789*, *794*, and *823*, measurements for the two larger groups (from pits *789* and *794*) are presented separately. Flakes from 5m squares 215 515 and 230 520 were added together to provide some comparison between stratified and residual and unstratified material. The characteristics of the flakes from the two squares are not, however, identical, and are recorded separately in Tables 5 and 6 (microfiche). Retouched pieces are recorded in Table 1 and in Table 2 (microfiche) in terms of the categories listed in Table 7 (microfiche). Selected forms are further described below.

Table 1. Composition and incidence of lithic material (summary).

	Cores	Irregular waste	Flakes	Chisel arrowheads	?Chisel arrowheads	Flake scrapers	Other scrapers	Borers	Straight-edged flake knife	Backed knife	Notch	Denticulate	Saws	Serrated pieces	Miscellaneous re-touched pieces	'Fabricator'	Axe or adze	Totals	'Pot-boilers'	Burnt flint (reddened)	Burnt sandstone	Burnt quartzite	Unburnt sandstone	Unburnt igneous rock	Drawings
Prehistoric pit groups																									
contexts 318, 319, 327, 338	33	41	837	1	1	4	2	1						5	3			928	1	2	2	4			F1-F6
contexts 789, 794, 823	45	89	1852		1	7	1	2		1	1			4	3			2005	12		11	3	1	1	F7-F18
Totals for pit groups	78	130	2689	1	1	11	3	3		1	1			9	6			2933	13	2	13	7	1	1	
Other contexts																									
in 5m square 215515	10	16	197			4							1	1	2			231							
in 5m square 230520	3	4	130	1		1		2							1			142							
remainder	46	30	1275	8	1	30	7	4	1			1	2	12	19	1	1	1439							F19-F25, SI
Totals for other contexts	59	50	1602	9	1	35	7	6	1			1	3	13	22	1	1	1811							
Totals for excavated area	137	180	4291	10	2	46	10	9	1	1	1	1	3	22	28	1	1	4744	13	2	13	7	1	1	
Drawings	F7-F11, F19	F12		F1, F20-F22	F2	F3, F4, F13, F14	F5	F6, F15	F23	F16	F17			F18, F24		F25	S1								

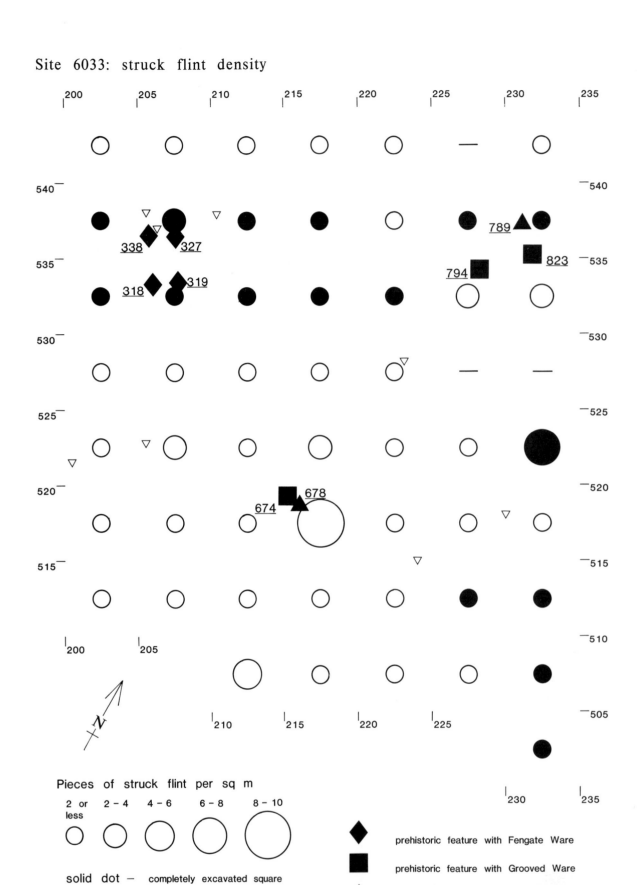

Figure 26 Diagramatic representation of struck flint density, expressed in number of pieces per square metre, in non-prehistoric contexts in each 5m square or part of 5m square, in relation to prehistoric features. Contexts spanning more than one 5m square are attributed to the square in which their greater part lay.

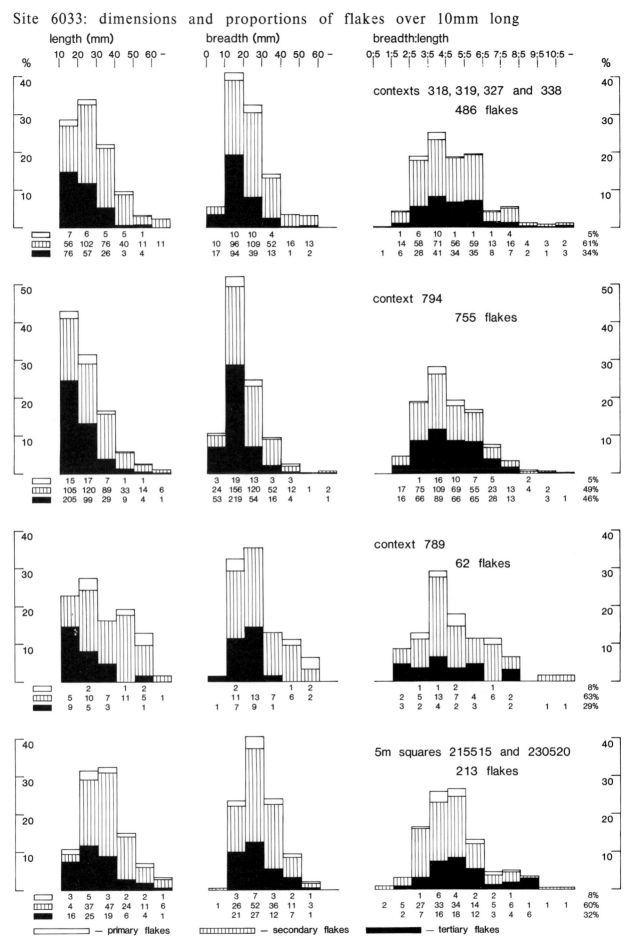

Figure 27 Dimensions and proportions of complete, unretouched flakes over 10mm long from selected prehistoric features (*318 + 319 + 327 + 338, 794, 789*), and from non-prehistoric contexts in 5m squares 215 515 and 230 520.

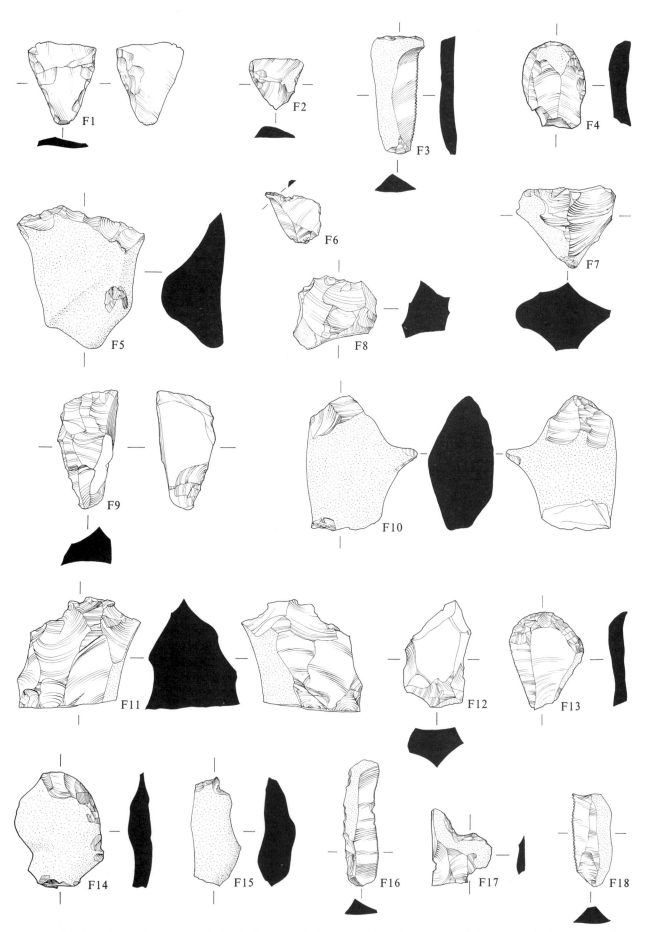

Figure 28 Struck flint from Later Neolithic features. F1–F6 from pits *327*, and *338*, F7–F18 from pits *789* and *794*. Unshaded areas represent thermally fractured surfaces. Scale 1:2.

	Cores	Irregular waste	Flakes	Retouched pieces	Totals
Prehistoric pit groups					
Pits *318, 319, 327, 338*	33 3.6%	41 4.4%	837 90.2%	17 1.8%	928
Pits *789, 794, 823*	45 2.2%	89 4.4%	1852 92.4%	19 1%	2005
Other contexts					
in 5m square *215515*	10 4.3%	16 6.9%	197 85.3%	8 3.5%	231
in 5m square *230520*	3 2.1%	4 2.8%	130 91.6%	5 3.5%	142
remainder	46 3.2%	30 2.1%	1275 88.6%	87 6.1%	1439

Table 3. Overall composition

Chisel arrowheads (F1, ?F2, F20, F21, F22), when they can be classified, are most frequently of Clark's (1934) form D (*e.g.* F20, F21; (Table 8 (microfiche)). The only stratified example (F1) is of form C. Insofar as the blanks on which they were made can be determined, these were all tertiary flakes, most of them from multi-platform cores, although a few, including the blank of F1, could have been struck from single-platform cores. At least two (F21 and F22) were made on flakes from Levallois- like cores, such as F19, which was itself found in the immediate area of pits *318, 319, 327,* and *338,* or another unillustrated example from context *738* in 5m square 215 515. As well as the ten bifacially-flaked chisel arrowheads, there are two unifacially-flaked pieces of similar size and outline (*e.g.* F2), which are listed as '?chisel arrowheads' in Tables 1 and 2 and as 'unifacial' in Table 8. The eight chisel arrowheads which can be plotted with any precision have a diffuse distribution, unrelated to each other or to prehistoric features.

Flake scrapers (F3, F4, F13, F14) are the most numerous class of retouched piece and end scrapers are the most numerous form among them (Table 9 (microfiche)). They are generally large. The seven complete flake scrapers from prehistoric contexts are between 30 and 80mm long, 20 and 50mm broad, and 7 and 17mm thick; and most of the scrapers from non-prehistoric contexts fall within the same size range (Table 10 (microfiche)). They are, in other words, made on blanks much larger than most of the unretouched flakes from the site (Figure 27).

Serrated pieces (*e.g.* F3 (also a scraper), F18, F24) are almost all, regardless of context, made on blades or blade-like flakes. The two exceptions are F24 and an unillustrated example found unstratified in 5m square 200 520.

Discussion
1. Flint-working. There is little doubt that the quantities of very small, sharp, fresh flakes, generally less than 10mm long (= chips), recovered from pits *327, 338, 789, 794,* and *823* are knapping debris. They were particularly numerous in pit *794,* where they amounted to approximately two-thirds of the flakes present. The sharpness, small size and inherent uselessness of this material means that it is unlikely to have been transported far from where it was generated. Potentially hazardous flint waste may have been deliberately placed in pits, together with smaller quantities of bone, pottery and other material. Alternatively, knappers may have actually worked over the pits, into which other domestic debris was also discarded.

The respective sizes of primary, secondary, and tertiary flakes from both groups of pits (Figure 27) are also indicative of *in situ* knapping, reflecting the removal of larger primary and secondary flakes prior to that of smaller tertiary flakes as the raw material was reduced. Low percentages of retouched pieces in the same contexts (Table 3) are consistent with this interpretation. It is not possible to distinguish stages in the knapping process in the three layers of pit *789* or the two layers of pit *794,* because relatively little flint was present in the first and because 96% of the abundant flint from the second was excavated from the lower layer (Table 2 (microfiche)). Context *794* has a particularly high percentage of tertiary flakes (Figure 27), likely to represent a later stage in the knapping process or the working of larger blocks of raw material.

The proportions of the flakes from pit *789,* which contained no pottery, are sufficiently similar to those of the flakes from those that did to suggest a comparable Later Neolithic date, given a general tendency to broad, squat proportions among the flakes of contemporary and later industries (Pitts 1978). The slightly larger size of its flakes is probably due to its fill not having been sieved, unlike the prolific parts of the fills of pits *327* and *794* (Table 2 (microfiche)). Flakes from non-prehistoric contexts in 5m squares 215 515 and 230 520 are almost certainly larger for the same reason.

2. ?Hearths. Burnt sandstone and quartzite fragments are concentrated in a single feature within each group of pits: in pit *327* in the north-east group and in pit *794* in the north-west (Table 2 (microfiche)). In each case, the remains of a hearth seems to have been deposited in the pit, especially as, in addition to the burnt material recorded in the final columns of Tables 1 and 2, fourteen pieces of struck flint from pit *327* and 105 from pit *794* were burnt, and as pit *794* also contained charcoal.

3. Affinities. The lithic material from both groups of pits, whether associated with Fengate Ware (*318, 319, 327, 338*) or with Grooved Ware (*794, 823,* and, by juxtaposition, *789*), has many of the characteristics of Later Neolithic industries from other sites in East Anglia (Healy 1985), in the form of proportionately broad flakes (Figure 27), relatively large flake scrapers (Table 10 (microfiche)), and a common range of retouched forms (Table 1). In particular, the association of one and possibly two chisel arrowheads (F1, F2) with Fengate Ware in pit *338* conforms to a widely observed association of chisel arrowheads with pottery of the Peterborough tradition and with Grooved Ware of the Woodlands substyle (Manby 1974, 84; Green 1980, 108, 235–6).

The material from both groups differs from most contemporary East Anglian industries in relatively low percentages of keeled (class D and E) cores, most of the cores from the pits being either single-platform (class A) or unclassifiable, generally because they are fragmentary (Table 4). This may reflect the specialised character of the material in the pits. Keeled cores are much more frequent

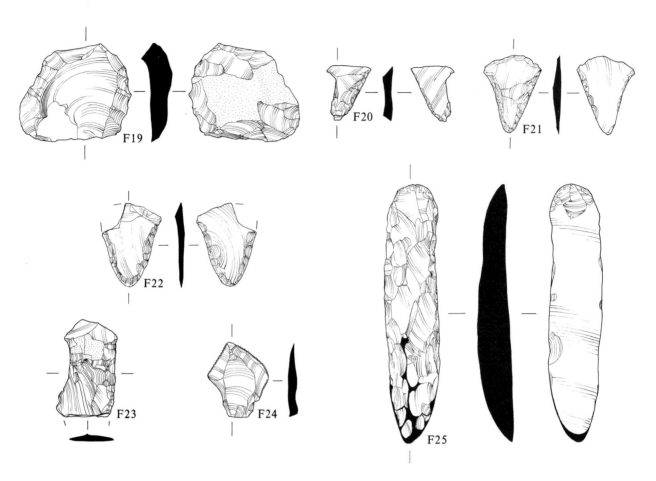

Figure 29 Struck flint from non-prehistoric contexts. F25 was found immediately above the fill of pit *338* and probably derived from it. Unshaded areas represent thermally fractured surfaces. Scale 1:2.

	A1	A2	B1	B2	B3	C	D	E	Levallois	Unclassified/ Fragmentary	Totals	Drawing
Prehistoric pit groups												
pits *318, 319, 327, 338*	-	9 27.3%	2 6.1%	1 3%	1 3%	2 6.1%	4 12.1%	-	-	14 42.4%	33	
pits *789, 794, 823*	-	10 22.2%	-	4 8.9%	6 13.3%	4 8.9%	5 11.1%	2 4.4%	-	14 31.2%	45	F7-F11
Other contexts												
in 5m square 2155515	-	2	-	-	-	-	2	2	1	3	10	
in 5m square 230520	-	-	1	-	-	-	1	-	-	1	3	
remainder	-	5	1	1	3	2	12	7	1	14	46	F19
Totals for other contexts	-	7 11.9%	2 3.4%	1 1.7%	3 5%	2 3.4%	15 25.4%	9 15.3%	2 3.4%	18 30.5%	59	
Drawings		F7				F8 F9	F10	F11	F19			

Cores are classified according to the scheme used for the Hurst Fen, Suffolk, industry (Clark 1960, 216), with the addition of Levallois cores. Blade scars are present on three cores, all from non-prehistoric contexts. Mean weight of complete cores from pits: *318, 319, 327, 338* = 168.4g; *789, 794, 823* = 68g.

Table 4. Cores

Drawing No.	Small Find No.	Description and comments	Context
F1		Chisel arrowhead of Clark's (1934) form C	338
F2		? chisel arrowhead, unifacially retouched only, as is a second example from context 218 in 5m square 200530.	338
F3		End scraper on serrated blade	342 (N half of fill of 327)
F4		Side-end scraper	338
F5		Scraper on thermally fractured fragment. Also a second, very similar example from the same context.	342
F6		Piercer, made by unilateral retouch on one edge of a pre-existing point	327
F7		Class A2 core with prepared platform	796 (lower fill of 794)
F8		Class C core	796
F9		Class C core	796
F10		Class D core	796
F11		Class E core	796
F12		Fragment of irregular waste	796
F13		End scraper	796
F14		Side-end scraper	796
F15		Piercer made on fragment of irregular waste	784
F16		Backed knife made by semi-abrupt retouch along the left edge of a blade. Heavy use-wear, approximating to Smith's (1965, 92) class A utilization, along right edge.	795 (W half of upper fill of 794)
F17		Notch	796
F18		Serrated blade	796
F19		Struck Levallois core, found unstratified in the area of pits 318, 319, 327 and 338.	317
F20		Chisel arrowhead of Clark's (1934) form D	153
F21		Chisel arrowhead of Clark's (1934) form D	778
F22	421	Fragmentary chisel arrowhead	363
F23		Fragmentary straight-edged flake knife	592
F24		Serrated flake	177
F25	408	End-polished 'fabricator'. Polish possibly the result of wear, possibly of deliberate finishing. Almost certainly derived from pit 338, since it was found immediately above the fill of this feature during its initial definition.	317
S1	33	Fragment from cutting edge of stone axe, heavily battered. Petrology no.N259. Group I.	4

Table 11. Catalogue of illustrated lithic material.

among the remainder of the material from the excavated area (Table 4), but were comparably scarce among the knapping debris of a Later Neolithic chipping floor on the edge of the 1971 shaft at Grime's Graves, Weeting-with-Broomhill, 17km to the west (Site 5640; Saville 1981b, 45).

Lithic material from non-prehistoric contexts may have accumulated over a long period and may not relate to the contents of the pits. The bulk of it has, however, a homogeneous aspect, compatible with a Later Neolithic date. The proportions of unretouched flakes from 5m squares 215 515 and 230 520 (Figure 27) are, like those of the flakes from the pits, comparable with those of Later Neolithic and subsequent industries in southern and eastern England (Pitts 1978). This sample is almost certainly representative of the remainder of the material from non-prehistoric contexts, among which blades, in the visual sense of proportionately narrow, parallel-sided flakes, are rare and only three of the forty-six cores have blade scars (Table 4). The range of retouched forms found in non-prehistoric contexts differs little from that found in prehistoric ones (Table 1) and is consistent with that found in other Later Neolithic industries. The rare stratified parallels for F25, an end-ground 'fabricator' found immediately above the fill of pit 338, tend to occur in Later Neolithic contexts, like one associated with Grooved ware and charcoal dated to 3680 ± 80 BP (BM-2265; 2320–1880 cal. BC) and 3740 ± 50 BP (BM-2206; 2320–2030 cal. BC) in the ditch of the Whitton Hill 1 enclosure,

Northumberland (Weyman 1985, fig. 4:2). The stone axe fragment, S1, although a surface find, may be broadly contemporary. Group I implements seem to have been distributed widely and on a large scale in the Later Neolithic (Smith 1979, 17–18) and are frequent in the East Anglian Breckland and on the adjoining fen edge (Clough and Cummins 1988, map 2).

Some relationship between the remainder of the material and the activity represented by the contents of the pits is thus possible. It is remarkable that chisel arrowheads, the form of projectile head consistently associated with the two pottery styles present in the pits, are the only form found among the remainder of the material, when all types of flint arrowhead, including forms regularly associated with other contemporary pottery styles, are densely concentrated in the Breckland (Green 1980, figs 31, 40, 41, 47). Most notable is the absence from the excavated area of oblique arrowheads, regularly associated with the Durrington Walls substyle of Grooved Ware (Manby 1974, 84; Green 1980, 235), and of barbed and tanged arrowheads, regularly associated with Beaker (Green 1980, 243–5). Also absent or scarce are other features of Beaker-associated industries, such as the practice of scale-flaking, especially on various knife forms, and the prevalence of small, 'thumbnail' scrapers (Healy 1986). The material from the excavated area stands out in this respect from the great surface collections made in the Breckland early in this century before afforestation was complete, which often include such elements, as does

Pottery

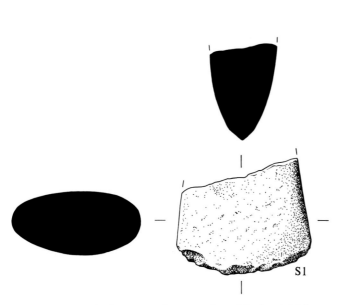

Figure 30 Stone axe fragment found during initial surface collection. Scale 1:2.

the excavated material from Fison Way, Thetford (Site 5853; Healy 1992). It is thus possible that the bulk of the lithic material from the excavation may derive from the same broad phase of Later Neolithic activity as the contents of the pits.

The overall density of 3.75 pieces of struck flint per m^2 of excavated area (Table 1) is a minimum one, which would be increased by an unknown factor if all archaeological and superficial deposits had been excavated. It is little more than half the density of approximately 6.2 pieces per m^2 calculated for surface material alone by W.G. Clarke and W.A. Dutt in 1905 on a plot of land in Inkerman Breck, Santon (now Lynford), then one of the prime collecting areas of the region (Clarke and Hewitt 1914, 432). Both emphasise how prolific of struck flint the Breckland has been: even the minimum figure for Harling is more than twice that of 1.6 pieces per m^2 for the Neolithic settlement on Broome Heath, Ditchingham (Site 10602), calculated by Bamford (1985, table 14), where pits were far more frequent than at Harling (Wainwright 1972, fig. 2).

Relatively high density goes with low proportions of retouched pieces: percentages of 1.8% and 1% for the two groups of pits (Table 3) are at the bottom of the ranges for industries from a number of Neolithic enclosures and settlements (Bamford 1985, table 14) and for a wider selection of Neolithic and Bronze Age industries (Healy 1993, table 53). This is consistent with interpretation of the pits' contents as predominantly knapping debris. A higher percentage of 5.5% for non-prehistoric contexts at Harling is almost certainly the product of the partial sieving of the material from the pits (Table 2 (microfiche)) and of the suggested deliberate disposal of small, sharp knapping debris in them, both of which would make for higher proportions of unretouched flakes. A tentative conclusion is that flint-knapping may have been a major, if not the major, activity carried out within the excavated area, and that the collection and working of local surface flint may have been a reason for its occupation.

Pottery

Description

The composition and incidence of prehistoric pottery are set out in Table 12. Selected sherds are illustrated in Figures 31–32 and described in Table 13.

1. ?Neolithic Bowl (P1). The form of P1 suggests that it was part of a plain Neolithic Bowl, although its hard, flint- and sand-tempered fabric is also compatible with those of local Late Bronze/Early Iron Age or full Iron Age wares. Nine plain body sherds of comparable fabric were found scattered over the excavated area (Fig. 26) and are listed as 'indeterminate prehistoric' in Table 12.

2. Fengate Ware (P2–11). Later Neolithic pottery of this style was recovered from pits *318, 319, 327,* and *338.* Sherds of P2 were found in *318* and *327,* and sherds of P4 in *319* and *338,* indicating that at least these pairs of pits, and probably the whole group, were open at the same time. It is characterized by predominantly grog- and sand-tempered fabrics, in which flint is sometimes present in varying quantities, with buff-to-orange outer, and sometimes inner, surfaces and grey cores (Table 13). Texture varies from relatively hard and sound (*e.g.* P2, P7) to coarse and friable (*e.g.* P3–5, P10). Surfaces of coarser sherds are sometimes pitted by the erosion of large pieces of grog (*e.g.* P3–4).

At least nine pots are represented (P2–9, P11). P10, although only a small body sherd, almost certainly represents a tenth, since its cord-impressed decoration is unmatched among the more complete vessels. All five rims (P2, P7–9, P11) have herring-bone decoration on the internal bevel, executed by finger-pinching or fingernail-impression on P2, P8–9 and perhaps on P11. There are two main forms: P11 is an almost complete flat-based bowl; P3–6 and P8 all seem to have come from jars with straight or slightly flaring walls. The collared rims of P5 and P8, and probably of P4, suggest that the remaining collar fragments (P7 and P9) may have come from similarly-shaped pots. Decorative techniques include finger-tip and fingernail impression (P4–9, P11), incision (P9, P11), twisted cord impression (P10), and the drawing of what appears to have been a smooth-toothed comb over the surface (P3, P6). Closely-spaced fingernail impressions are used to produce continuous or almost continuous lines on the collars of P8 and P9 and in part of the decoration of P11. Motifs are simple, with the outstanding exception of P11, which combines a maze of intersecting oblique lines with a pair of more emphatically-executed lozenges.

3. Grooved Ware (P12–14). Small quantities of Grooved Ware were recovered from pits *674, 794* and *823.* The sherds from each are in a different fabric, tempered respectively with flint and sand, a vanished calcareous or organic filler, and sand alone. The sherds of P12 and P14 are relatively hard and sound, those of P13 soft and friable. The material is very fragmentary. Decoration consists of apparently pinched-up cordons (P12–13), converging into a 'knot' on P12, incised slashes (P12), lines (P14) and herring-bone decoration (P14), impressed dots (P14), and an applied clay pellet (P14).

Other Later Neolithic/Early Bronze Age pottery (P15). This consists of six small, abraded, predominantly grog-tempered sherds from non-prehistoric contexts. Where decoration survives it consists in three cases of

	?Neolithic Bowl		Fengate Ware		Grooved Ware		Other Later Neolithic/Early Bronze Age		Indeterminate Prehistoric		Drawings
	sherds	wt.(g)	sherds	wt.(g)	sherds	wt.(g)	sherds	wt.(g)	sherds	wt.(g)	
Prehistoric pits											
318			1	40							P2
319			3	85							P3, P4
327 (inc. *342*)			31	645							P2, P5-P11
338			13	95							P4
674					4	15					P12
794 (from lower layer *796*)					10	15					P13
823					1	8					P14
Other contexts											
103									1	5	
127									1	5	
153									1	20	
208	1	20									P1
249									1	10	
317							3	25	1	10	P15
330							1	10			
390									1	5	
497									1	15	
545									1	15	
645							2	10			
739									1	15	
Totals	1	20	48	865	15	38	6	45	9	100	
Drawings	P1		P2-P11		P12-P14		P15				
Overall total: 79 sherds, weighing 1068g											

Table 12. Prehistoric pottery

incised or grooved lines, as on P15 and two unillustrated sherds, and in the fourth case of rows of indeterminate impressions.

Discussion
1. Affinities. P1, if it is indeed of Earlier Neolithic date, is too fragmentary to be ascribed to any particular Bowl style. The tradition as a whole is represented within the Breckland by sherds from pits at Brettenham, 4km downstream to the south-west (Site 5653; Healy 1984a, fig. 5.3), Ickburgh, 21km to the north-west (Site 11771), and Fison Way, Thetford, 12km to the west (Site 5853; Healy 1992), as well as by material sealed beneath a barrow at Eriswell (Dymond 1973, 10–15) and by pottery associated with the first phase of Swale's Tumulus, Worlington (Briscoe 1957, 107–9), both in Suffolk. Stray finds have been made at Grime's Graves, 17km to the west (Site 5640; Longworth 1981, 39; Longworth, Ellison and Rigby 1988, 12), Shropham, 9km to the north (Site 9027; Healy 1984 b) and Saham Toney, 19km to the north-east (Site 8747; Healy 1984b), as well as at Foxhole Heath, Eriswell (Briscoe 1954, 18, fig. 4:c) and Bombay Cottage, Mildenhall (Leaf 1935, 108, fig. 6:30) in Suffolk.

P2–10 conform to Smith's (1956, 106–16) definition of Fengate Ware, in features such as collared, internally bevelled rims (P5, P7, P8–9), cylindrical or flaring bodies (P3–6, P8), finger-tip-impressed pits in the neck (P4–5), and fingernail-impressed and linear decoration on the body (P2–6, P8). The only major characteristic of the style which is absent is a nearly conical outline in which the walls taper to an unstably narrow base.

The combed decoration of P3 and P6 is more readily paralleled among Grooved Ware than among Fengate Ware, as at Durrington Walls, Wiltshire (Longworth 1971, 69–70, fig. 55: P401–2). Links with the Grooved Ware tradition are more pronounced in P11 which was, on the evidence of context, fabric, rim form, and rim decoration, made and used with Fengate Ware vessels P2–10. Its external decoration may be compared with that of a Grooved Ware bowl from Runton (Site 6370; Gell 1949, fig. 1), and with the internal decoration of another from the basal deposits of the 1971 shaft at Grime's Graves (Longworth 1981, fig. 22). Its form is matched in several other bowls from the site (Smith 1915, 208–10; Longworth, Ellison and Rigby 1988, figs 4–6). Bowls are also present, but less frequent, in other Grooved Ware assemblages, among them that of the Storey's Bar Road subsite at Fengate, Cambridgeshire (Pryor 1978, fig. 37:10). The paired lozenges of P11, more deeply incised and impressed than the rest of its decoration, recall the repertoire of motifs common to Grooved Ware and to other contemporary media, including both small, portable objects and the stones of megalithic structures (Clarke, Cowie and Foxon 1985, 56–57; pls 3.17, 3.18, 3.37, 3.48, 5.7, 7.20).

Fengate Ware is locally rare (Cleal 1984, fig. 9.3). The Harling assemblage as a whole is best matched by that from Icklingham in the Suffolk Breckland, 23km to the south-west, from which Piggott illustrates several sherds (1931, fig. 17) and a restored pot (1954, pl. X:2). The predominantly grog- and sand-tempered sherds represent at least eight Fengate style pots, which share with the

41

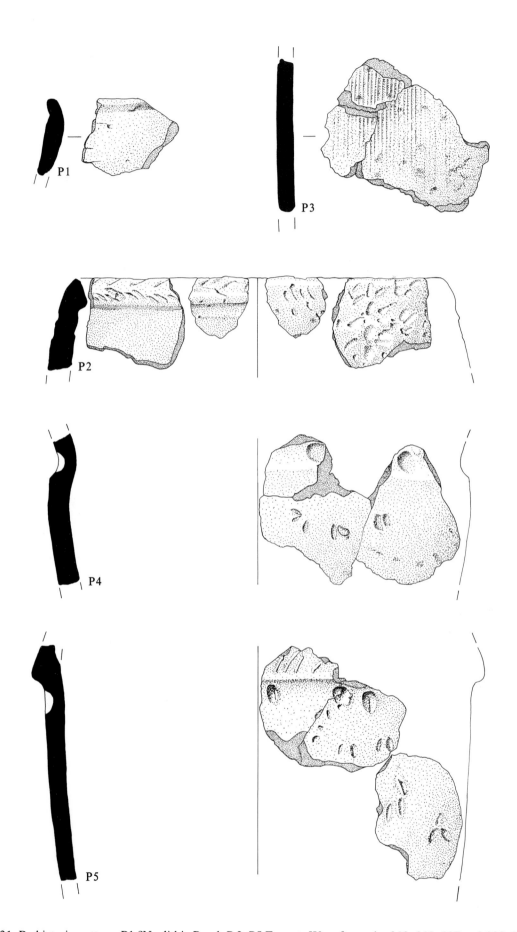

Figure 31 Prehistoric pottery: P1 ?Neolithic Bowl; P 2–P5 Fengate Ware from pits *318, 319, 327* and *338*. Scale 1:2.

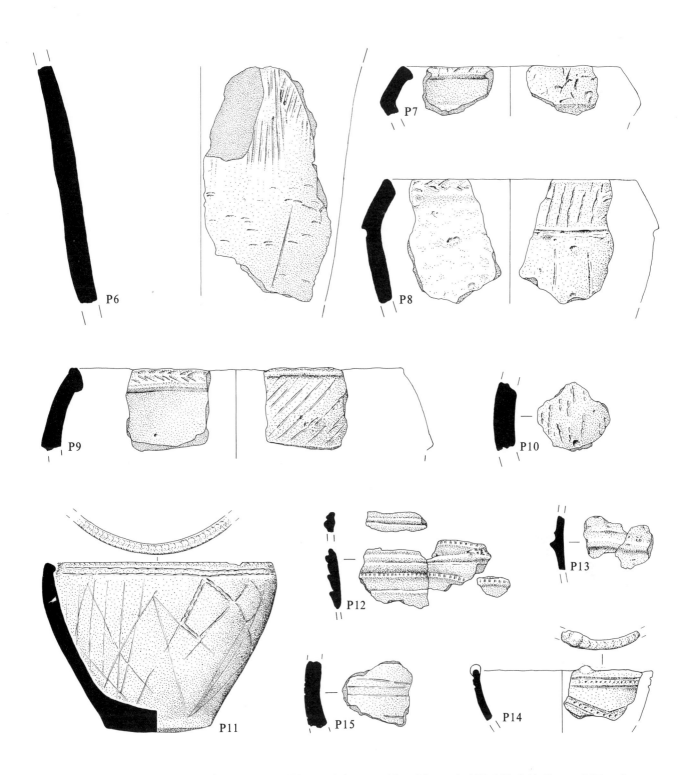

Figure 32 Prehistoric pottery: P6–P11 Fengate Ware and decorated bowl from pit *327*; P12–P14 Grooved Ware from pits *674, 794* and *823*; P15 indeterminate Later Neolithic or Early Bronze Age. Scale 1:2.

Drawing No.	Style/date	Hardness	Texture	Filler(s) at x30 magnification	Colour			Decoration	Comments	Context(s)
					int.	core	ext.			
P1	?Neolithic Bowl	hard	coarse	flint with some sand	7.5YR 4/2 brown-grey	7.5YR 4/0 grey-brown	7.5YR 5/2 buff-brown		Diameter at max. extent of sherd 18cm. Pitch uncertain	208
P2	Fengate Ware	hard	coarse	flint with some sand	7.5YR 5/4 buff	5YR 3/1 grey	5YR 4/3 orange-grey	finger-pinching	Smaller sherd (from context 327) very weathered	318, 327
P3	Fengate Ware	soft	coarse	grog with some chalk and some sand	7.5YR 4/4 brown	7.5YR 4/0 grey	7.5YR 4/6 buff-orange	?combing	Apparently straight-sided. Approx. diameter 30cm. Much weathered.	319
P4	Fengate Ware	soft	coarse	grog with some sand	7.5YR 5/4 buff	7.5YR 4/0 grey	7.5YR 5/4 buff	finger-tip impression, finger-pinching		319, 338
P5	Fengate Ware	soft	coarse	grog with some sand and some flint	7.5YR 6/6 buff	7.5YR 6/0 grey	7.5YR 5/4 buff	fingernail impression, finger-tip impression, finger-pinching	Collared sherd very leached.	327, 342
P6	Fengate Ware	medium	medium	sand with some grog	5YR 4/1 grey	5YR 4/1 grey	5YR 4/6 red-brown	combing, finger-nail impression		327
P7	Fengate Ware	hard	medium	sand	7.5YR 5/4 buff	7.5YR 4/0 grey	7.5YR 5/2 buff-grey	fingernail impression		327
P8	Fengate Ware	medium	medium	grog with some flint and some sand	7.5YR 6/2 grey-buff	7.5YR 5/0 grey	7.5YR 5/6 buff-orange	finger-pinching, fingernail impression, channelling		342
P9	Fengate Ware	medium	medium	sand	7.5YR 7/4 buff	7.5YR 4/0 grey	7.5YR 6/4 buff	fingernail impression, other impression, incision		342
P10	Fengate Ware	soft	coarse	grog with some sand	5YR 6/1 grey	5YR 5/1 grey	5YR 6/3 buff-pink	twisted cord impression		342
P11	Fengate Ware	medium	medium	grog and sand	7.5YR 5/0 grey-buff	7.5YR 3/0 grey	7.5YR 5/4 buff-grey	incision, fingernail impression	As much as possible of the exterior of the pot is illustrated, to show the irregularity of its decoration.	327
P12	Grooved Ware (Woodlands)	medium	medium	flint with some sand	7.5YR 4/2 grey-buff	7.5YR 3/0 grey	7.5YR 5/4 buff-grey	pinched-up ridges and 'knot', incision	Diameter ?13cm	674
P13	Grooved Ware	soft	coarse	vacuoles	5YR 4/2 grey-buff	5YR 4/1 grey	5YR 5/2 buff-grey	pinched-up ridges	Also 7 smaller sherds, not illustrated	796
P14	Grooved Ware (Woodlands)	medium	fine	sand	7.5YR 6/4 buff	7.5YR 6/0 grey	7.5YR 6/4 buff	impression, incision, appliqué	Rim-top decoration very abraded	823
P15	Later Neo/EBA	soft	coarse	grog with some sand and some flint	5YR 3/1 grey	5YR 4/1 grey-brown	5YR 6/6 buff-orange	incision		317

Table 13. Catalogue of illustrated prehistoric pottery

44

Harling material such features as collared rims with decorated internal bevels, finger-pitted hollow necks, deep, jar-like forms, and incised lattice decoration. One and possibly two (Piggott 1931, fig. 17:1,2) may be reconstructed as bowls of similar form to P11. The finger-pinched and fingernail-impressed decoration of many of the Harling pots is, however, lacking.

P12 is certainly of Grooved Ware but is too fragmentary to be attributed to any particular substyle. P14–15, however, both conform to the Woodlands substyle (Wainwright and Longworth 1971, 238–40) in features such as the applied clay pellet and herring-bone decoration on the rim of P14 and the plain and slashed cordons and 'knot' of P12. Grooved Ware is locally abundant (Cleal 1984, fig. 9.4), occurring within the Breckland at Grime's Graves, (Longworth 1981, 39; Longworth, Ellison and Rigby 1988, figs 4–6) and Thetford (Site 5815; Healy 1984 a, fig. 5.10; Site 5853; Healy 1992) in Norfolk and at Honington (Fell 1951), two sites in West Stow (Wainwright and Longworth 1971, 286–7; Martin 1979), and two sites in Pakenham (Wainwright and Longworth 1971, 286; Martin, Plouviez and Feldman 1986, 153–4) in Suffolk. There are also two Grooved Ware sherds among the Icklingham material described above (Wainwright and Longworth 1971, 285). The Woodlands substyle is particularly well-represented at Honington, where the features of P12 and P14 are closely matched (Fell 1951, fig. 9).

2. Dating. The currency of Neolithic Bowl pottery is defined by the radiocarbon dates assembled by Herne (1988, table 2.2), which indicate a *floruit* spanning the fourth millennium cal. BC. P1, if it is to be attributed to this tradition, may thus derive from an earlier episode of activity than the stratified prehistoric pottery from the site.

The uncertain dating of Fengate Ware is somewhat clarified by a radiocarbon determination of 4520 ± 80 BP (OxA-3578; 3500–2925 cal. BC) made on organic residue from the interior surface of a Fengate Ware vessel from the base of the outer ditch of a small, perhaps funerary, ovoid enclosure at Lower Horton, Berkshire and confirmed by others on samples from the same stratigraphic horizon (Ford forthcoming). Although surprising early, it can be seen as reinforcing Smith's view of the development of the Peterborough Ware tradition from the Neolithic Bowl tradition (1974, 111–3). So too can the position of the vessel in a monument analogous to small, late, long barrows, with plain Neolithic Bowl and Ebbsfleet Ware in its earlier, inner ditch. The span of the style, however, remains uncertain. There is a rather later determination of 4080 ± 130 BP (HAR-1451; 2920–2290 cal. BC) for charcoal from a pit at Thirlings, Northumberland, which contained pottery with some Fengate-like characteristics (Miket 1976, 119, figs 7.10–11).

Given the similarity of decoration between P11 and one of the Grooved Ware dishes from the 1971 shaft at Grime's Graves, radiocarbon dates for the basal deposits in which the latter were found may be relevant. They are 3781 ± 67 BP (BM-778; 2460–2030 cal. BC) and 3789 ± 60 BP (BM-776; 2460–2110 cal. BC). The numerous radiocarbon determinations for the southern variants of Grooved Ware, including the Woodlands substyle, cluster in the mid to late third millennium cal. BC (Healy 1984a, 112).

Conclusions

Whatever the original function or functions of the pits, they were ultimately filled with debris, including broken pottery, the remains of hearths and, in the case of pit *794*, charcoal and a small quantity of animal bone. It is argued above that most of the material from pits *327, 338, 789, 794,* and *823* consists of deliberately deposited knapping debris, and that flint-knapping may have been a major activity within the excavated area. Cleal suggests (1984, 148–151) that the contents of several Later Neolithic pits, most of them including Grooved Ware, in East Anglia may be most readily interpreted as formal deposits. This may extend to pits *327, 338, 789, 794,* and *823,* given their regular, quadrangular arrangement (Fig. 7) and the exceptional character of P11.

It is impossible to tell whether the contents of the pits and the remainder of the material represent a single episode or many. Pits *318, 319, 327,* and *338* may reasonably be assumed to have been filled in at the same time. Pits *789, 794,* and *823,* however, are related only by proximity and by the presence in two of them of Grooved Ware sherds. The coincidence of *674* and *678* with the highest concentration of lithic material from non-prehistoric contexts (Fig. 26) suggests but does not demonstrate a relationship. The overlapping currencies of Fengate Ware and Grooved Ware mean that the north-east and north-west groups of pits could have been filled concurrently or at different times. The separate occurrence of potentially contemporary Later Neolithic and Early Bronze Age pottery styles is commonplace (Whittle 1981, 310–11; Cleal 1984, 138); its interpretation is problematical.

The area excavated was selected without reference to its potential for prehistoric occupation, although this proved considerable. A consequent question is whether similar results would be obtained by the excavation of an equivalent area in any comparable location in the Breckland. The record of surface finds from the region as a whole is massive, and the features and material recovered during the excavation are far from isolated in the immediate locality. Potentially contemporary sites and finds within a 2km radius of the excavated area include a Late style Beaker (Site 6023; Clarke 1970, corpus no. 522, fig. 877); Bronze Age sherds (Site 6013); a flanged copper alloy axe (Site 19569); four flint scatters (Sites 19834, 19837, 19839, 19840); two isolated flint axes (Sites 6024, 17717); four round barrows (Sites 6011 (Lawson 1986), 6104, 6105, 6114); and three pot-boiler concentrations, all with possibly associated struck flint (Sites 15841, 19698, 20358). The last two are on sand and gravel hillocks emerging from the peat of the Thet valley south of the excavated area (Fig. 1), where small quantities of struck flint are to be found on several other hillocks. There is a strong suggestion that the results obtained in the excavated area may be representative of the locality, or even of a large part of the region.

Such Neolithic and Early Bronze Age settlement as has been found in the Breckland, in the form of occupation sites and pottery finds, is riverine in distribution, exemplified by the location of Harling in the Thet valley, Icklingham and West Stow in the Lark valley and Honington and Pakenham on the Black Bourn. This reflects the absence of any accessible water supply other than rivers and meres in a region underlain by pervious sands and chalks. It has been suggested (Healy 1984a,

126–7) that, for geological reasons, most of the region may have been as unsuitable for agriculture in Neolithic and Bronze Age times as it is today, when extremely free drainage and one of the lowest average rainfalls in Britain result in frequent restriction of plant growth by drought (Corbett 1973, 19, tables 4 and 5). Its vast volume of lithic finds may reflect its use as pasture, hunting ground, and raw material source by communities whose more lasting settlements lay in adjoining regions. Its value as a raw material source is to be seen not only in its *in situ* flint deposits, mined at Grime's Graves and perhaps elsewhere, but also in its wealth of surface flint, such as was worked at Harling, which surpasses the gravel flint of adjoining regions in size and quality.

An intensification of Breckland raw material use in the Later Neolithic and Early Bronze Age may perhaps be related to the first appearance of pollen of plants associated with clearance at *c.* 3300 cal. BC in the sediments of Hockham Mere, 9.5km north-west of Harling (Bennett 1983, 482). Bennett suggests that the extent and permanence of Later Neolithic clearance in the Hockham Mere catchment may have been overestimated by Godwin and Tallantire (1951, 302–6) and Sims (1978, 58). He envisages only small, temporary clearings at this time, with significant clearances beginning only *c.* 750 cal. BC. If he is correct, and if the Hockham Mere catchment is representative of the region, then such small clearings may perhaps have been made on the more fertile and less excessively drained calcareous slope soils which Legge (1981, 93–4) suggests as the best-suited within the region to prehistoric agriculture and pasture.

Intensification of local activity in the Later Neolithic and Early Bronze Age, although not leading to permanent forest clearance, is indicated by the working of the flint mines at Grime's Graves from *c.* 2650 cal. BC to *c.* 2050 cal. BC (Burleigh *et al.* 1979, 47), by the predominantly contemporary character of the great surface collections, and by the dating of known settlements.

II. The Coins
by Marion M. Archibald

The Middle Harling Hoard
The following fifty-eight coins and two blanks were apparently dispersed from a single deposit. When the Middle Harling coins were published in Archibald 1985, the sceattas here numbered 61 and 63, and also the Beonnas 67 and 68, were believed to have derived from the hoard, but it has now been established that they were found too far from its nucleus for it to be likely that they could have been part of it (see plan of findspots, Fig. 33).

Abbreviations

BM	acquired by British Museum
CAM	acquired by Fitzwilliam Museum Cambridge
CAR	acquired by National Museum of Wales, Cardiff
PRIV	private collection

Sceattas (thick, small-flan, pennies): 7 coins
Runic legends as read by Professor R.I. Page. All are base silver; weights of most are affected by corrosion.

1. Series L. Diademed profile head to left +NNOONIA (retrograde, and some letters badly formed — devolved LVNDONIA)/man holding two crosses. Wt: 0.75g. (BM).
   SF 600. Context *850*, filling of ditch *661*.
2. Series R. Profile head to right, devolved runic inscription, 'epa'/devolved standard. Wt: 0.71g. (BM).

SF 282. Topsoil in excavation at 208/542.
3. Series R. Similar to previous except runic inscription, 'wigr'. Wt: 0.81g. (BM).
   SF 232. Topsoil in excavation at 221/541.
4. Series R. Similar to previous except runic inscription, 'wigrd'. Wt: 0.78g. (BM).
   SF 329. Context *153* at 210/528.
5. Series R. Similar to previous except runic inscription, 'tilber[l]t' (blundered 'tilberht'). Same obverse die as No.56 below. Wt: 0.83g. (BM).
   SF 438. Context *446* at 229/539.
6. Series R. Small, more realistic, profile head to right, runic inscription 'ti[.berht]'/devolved standard. Same obverse die as next. Wt: 0.51g (very corroded). (BM).
   SF 20. Topsoil in 1981 excavation.
7. Series R. Same obverse die as previous. Reverse die a more devolved form of the standard design, more analagous to that used on the Beonna coins by the moneyer Efe. Wt: 0.90g. (BM).
   SF 353. Context 153 at 212/531.

Beonna of East Anglia: 50 coins

Moneyer Efe: 37 coins
King's name and title, in mixed runes and Roman letters, around a central pellet or cross/cross motif within central square, lines extending from corners to outer circle; cross and letters of moneyer's name EFE (usually in Roman letters, but occasionally with a runic 'f'), and groups of pellets in each outer quadrant. The corpus number (Archibald 1985, C1–C75) is followed by the Small Find number.

8. 0.61g (BM) C1 SF 54 Brown soil in 1981 excavation.
9. 0.83g (BM) C2 SF 19 Topsoil, area of 1981 excavation.
10. 0.88g (BM) C3 SF 288 Topsoil in excavation at 211/543.
11. 0.90g (BM) C4 SF 324 Context *150* at 227/512.
12. 0.68g (BM) C5 SF 375 Context *211* at 220/536.
13. 1.05g (BM) C7 SF 23 Topsoil area of 1981 excavation.
14. 1.03g (BM) C8 SF 17 Topsoil area of 1981 excavation.
15. 1.00g (BM) C9 SF 28 Topsoil area of 1981 excavation.
16. 1.06g (BM) C10 SF 22 Topsoil area of 1981 excavation.
17. 1.13g (BM) C11 SF 29 Topsoil area of 1981 excavation.
18. 1.03g (BM) C12 SF 27 Topsoil area of 1981 excavation.
19. 0.97g (BM) C14 SF 38 Brown soil in 1981 excavation.
20. 1.05g (BM) C16 SF 18 Topsoil area of 1981 excavation.
21. 1.00g (BM) C17 SF 2 Topsoil area of 1981 excavation.
22. 1.03g (BM) C18 SF 8 Topsoil area of 1981 excavation.
23. 0.86g (BM) C20 SF 389 Context *238* at 212/533.
24. 0.99g (BM) C22 SF 16 Topsoil area of 1981 excavation.
25. 1.15g (BM) C23 SF 36 Brown soil in 1981 excavation.
26. 1.10g (BM) C24 SF 47 Topsoil area of 1981 excavation.
27. 0.96g (BM) C25 SF 55 Brown soil in 1981 excavation.
28. 1.04g (BM) C26 SF 222 Topsoil in excavation at 210/531.
29. 0.58g (BM) C29 SF 40 Brown soil in 1981 excavation.
30. 0.89g (BM) C30 SF 51 Brown soil in 1981 excavation.
31. 0.80g (BM) C32 SF 56 Brown soil in 1981 excavation.
32. 1.10g (BM) C33 SF 271 Topsoil in excavation at 222/535.
33. 1.01g (CAR) C34 SF 287 Topsoil in excavation at 214/544.
34. 0.81g (BM) C35 SF 419 Context *343*, filling of ditch *852*.
35. 0.93g (BM) C37 SF 7 Topsoil area of 1981 excavation.
36. 0.90g (BM) C38 SF 13 Topsoil area of 1981 excavation.
37. 0.83g (BM) C39 SF 30 Brown soil in 1981 excavation.
38. 1.00g (BM) C40 SF 4 Topsoil area of 1981 excavation.
39. 1.02g (BM) C41 SF 41 Brown soil in 1981 excavation.
40. 1.01g (CAM) C42 SF 404 Context *298* at 220/532.
41. 0.98g (BM) C44 SF 21 Topsoil area of 1981 excavation.
42. 0.98g (BM) C45 SF 46 Brown soil in 1981 excavation.
43. 0.89g (BM) C46 SF 1 Topsoil area of 1981 excavation.
44. 1.06g (BM) C47 SF 39 Brown soil in 1981 excavation.

Moneyer Wilred: 9 coins
King's name in runes, with single rune representing his title, around central pellet or cross/moneyer's name 'wilred' in runes around central pellet or cross. (King's name side abnormally the upper die, as also Interlace type below).

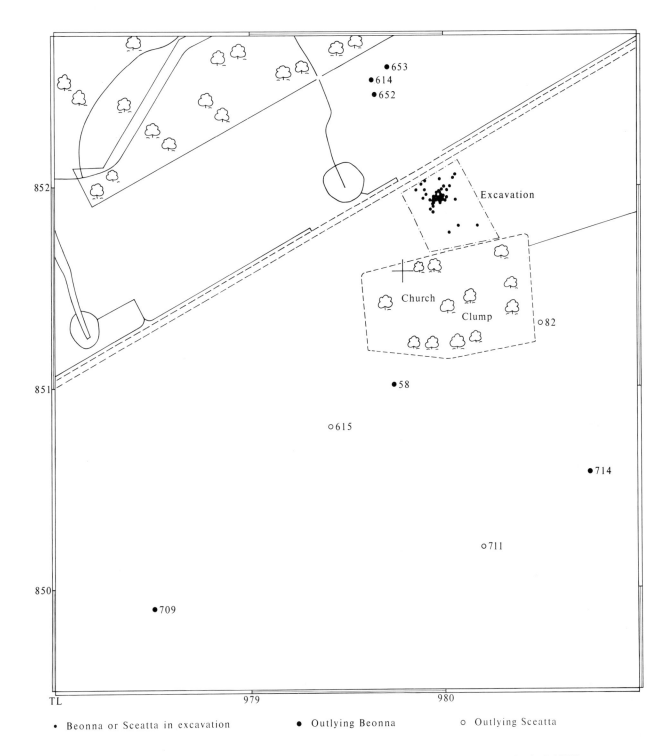

Figure 33 Distribution of Middle Saxon coins in excavation and surroundings. Scale 1:1875

Legend (below figure):
- Beonna or Sceatta in excavation
- Outlying Beonna
- Outlying Sceatta

45. 0.82g (BM) C52 SF 5 Topsoil area of 1981 excavation.
46. 1.01g (BM) C53 SF 6 Topsoil area of 1981 excavation.
47. 1.10g (BM) C54 SF 48 Brown soil in 1981 excavation.
48. 0.98g (BM) C55 SF 283 Topsoil in excavation at 212/540.
49. 0.89g (BM) C56 SF 3 Topsoil area of 1981 excavation.
50. 0.81g (BM) C60 SF 590 Filling of pit *800*.
51. 0.67g (BM) C62 SF 52 Brown soil in 1981 excavation.
52. 1.01g (BM) C63 SF 34 Brown soil in 1981 excavation.
53. 1.03g (BM) C66 SF 417 Context *341* at 216/530.
54. 0.87g (BM) C67 SF 280 Topsoil in excavation at 224/536.

Moneyer Werferth: 1 coin
King's name and title in mixed runes and Roman letters around a central pellet/pellet within pelleted annulet inside a square with a pellet in each angle with lines extending from the corners to the outer circle with a cross and the moneyer's name 'werferth' in runes in pairs in each outer quadrant.

55. 1.07g (BM) C69 SF 49 Brown soil in 1981 excavation.

No moneyer's name, Interlace type: 3 coins
King's name and title in runes around a central pellet/interlace pattern. (King's name side abnormally the upper die, as Wilred's above.)

56. 1.08g (BM) C72 SF 37 Brown soil in 1981 excavation.
57. 0.90g (CAM) C73 SF 370 Context *211* at 221/537.
58. 0.43g (BM) C74 SF 539 (fragment only) Context *692* at 213/516.

Blanks

These are flatter, thinner discs of silver showing the marks of hammering, but no designs or inscriptions. The silver is finer than that of all the 8th-century coins present.

59 0.85g and 0.83g (BM) SF 302 and 303. Found 0.3m apart in Context **and** *105* at 226/513.
60.
59. 0.85g (BM) Diameter 17mm SF 302.
60. 0.83g (BM) Diameter 19mm SF 303.

Note on the Hoard

Beonna became king of part of East Anglia when the kingdom was divided into three parts on the death of Alfwald, the last of the Wuffingas kings, in 749. Norman chronicles describe him as a contemporary of Offa of Mercia, 757–96, without giving any specific information on the length of his reign. Middle Harling is the only known hoard to include coins of Beonna, and it is particularly important in associating them with the base coins of other issues produced during the latest phase of the sceatta series. The Beonna coins of all types and moneyers present were in virtually unworn condition, suggesting that his coinage was of relatively short duration, and was struck in silver declining rapidly from *c.* 75% fine, through a 50% standard, to 25% or even less. The coins of the moneyer Efe display a sophisticated system of marking identifying individual dies by the number of pellets around the initial cross.

The moneyer Wilred also struck broad-flan, reformed, pennies in fine silver for Offa in East Anglia, and this is one of the reasons discussed in Archibald 1985 for dating Beonna's coinage, and the deposition of the hoard, to the troubled period following the death of Aethelbald of Mercia in 757, from which Offa emerged the victor, rather than any earlier in Beonna's reign.

The distribution pattern of finds of Beonna's coinage as known at present, including other isolated finds, shows a greater concentration of Efe's coins in the north, and of Wilred's coins in the south of East Anglia, suggesting possible different minting places; Thetford and Ipswich would appear to be the most likely candidates. The rare coins of Werferth are technologically associated with those of Efe, and so presumptively belong to Thetford. The almost equally rare coins with the Interlace cross type and no moneyer's name have affinities with the Wilred group, but seem at present to have a more central distribution, and might possibly be from a third minting place. The monastery at Beadricesworth (later Bury St Edmunds) has very tentatively, and more controversially, been suggested. More evidence of provenance is however required before the question of the location of minting places can be a matter of more than speculation.

Other Finds of Sceattas and Beonna Coins from Middle Harling

The following coins, although dating from the same period as those in the hoard, were found so far from the nucleus of the finds that it seems unlikely that they were part of it (see the plan of findspots, Fig. 33). Apart from Nos 61, 63, 67 and 68, they were discovered after the publication of the hoard in 1985. The Beonna die numbers quoted are those identified in Archibald 1985, with consecutive numbering for dies not recorded there.

61. **Series U.** (Published in Archibald 1985 as part of the hoard.) Kneeling man drawing a bow/bird to right, head turned back, *c.* 715–30. Wt: 1.03g. A coin of these types from different dies found

at Warbury Camp, Berks. (Rigold and Metcalf 1977, 49, pl. III, 44). (PRIV).
SF 615. Found in 1983 at TL 9794 8508.

62. **Sceat,** Series R, late very base derivative series, *c.* 730–55. Devolved profile bust to right/devolved standard. Wt: 1.07g (PRIV).
SF 711. Found in 1988 at TL 9820 8521.

63. **Series R.** (Published in Archibald 1985 as part of the hoard.) Similar to previous except runic inscription '[ti]lberlt', blundered 'tilberht'. Same obverse die as hoard coin No. 5 above. Wt: 0.59g (CAM).
SF 82. Found in 1981 at TL 9805 8513.

64. **Beonna.** Moneyer Efe, dies 1/22 in BNJ 1985 corpus. Wt: 0.75g (PRIV).
SF 652. Found in 1987 at TL 9796 8524 by Mr D. Bailey.

65. **Beonna.** Moneyer Efe, dies 3/29, unrecorded reverse die. Rev.: ..E.. F..E.. The reverse die was unrecorded and brings to eight the number of reverse dies used with obverse 3. Wt: 1.01g (PRIV).
SF 653. Found in 1987 at TL 9797 8526 by Mr D. Bailey.

66. **Beonna.** Moneyer Efe, dies 6/19 (die duplicate of one of the coins in the hoard, BNJ Corpus No.C45. Wt: 1.10g. (PRIV).
SF 714. Found in 1988 at TL 98075 85055.

67. **Beonna.** Moneyer Wilred. (Published in Archibald 1985 as part of the hoard, Corpus No. C59). 1.04g (CAM).
SF 58. Found in 1980 at TL 9797 8510.

68. **Beonna.** Moneyer Wilred. (Published in Archibald 1985 as part of the hoard, Corpus No. C64). 0.81g (PRIV).
SF 614. Found in 1983 at TL 9796 8525.

69. **Beonna.** Interlace type.
Obv.: +ben+na followed by the usual rune Ⴘ believed to be a bind-rune for REX; here it has, exceptionally, a pellet in the 'triangle' at the top. Rev.: Interlace, die 1. Wt: 1.11g (double-struck). The lay-out of the obverse with the king's name interrupted by a second cross, is unrecorded for the Interlace type, but is that already familiar from its use on the coins of the moneyer Wilred. The coin is on the broadest flan of all the known Beonnas, indicating that it is probably late in the series, and corrosion products suggest that the silver (not analysed) is probably base. (PRIV).
SF 709. Found in 1987 at TL 9785 8499.

Other Coins from Middle Harling

Celtic

70. **Base-metal core of a contemporary forgery of an Iron Age gold stater,** with a thin layer of gold adhering in places. The details of the types are uncertain, but are very close to those of Addedomarus (*cf.* Mack 256), but this coin does not appear to have been inscribed. The horse here faces towards the left, rather than towards the right as on the normal Mack type. Weight not recorded. Identification by Tony Gregory. (PRIV).
SF 607. Found in 1984 at TL 9788 8503.

Roman

71. **Domitian, 81–96** AD, sestertius. Identification by Tony Gregory. (PRIV).
SF 57. Found in 1980 south of Church Clump.

72. **Uncertain emperor.** A cut segment (less than half) of a very worn 1st-century sestertius, rev. type illegible. Wt: 8.43g. (BM).
SF 234. Topsoil in excavation at 205/540.

73. **Antoninus Pius, 138–61.** Dupondius, rev., Providentia, 155–8AD (BMC 2024), hole to left of head (or to right of rev. figure). Wt: 11.6g. (PRIV).
SF 88. Found in 1981 at TL 9797 8510.

74. **Antoninus Pius, 138–61** AD. A very worn as, with a crescent-shaped, 'bite' cut out of the edge. Reverse type illegible. Wt: 7.98g (BM).
SF 546. Context 712 at 207/520.

75. **Barbarous radiate.** Copy of a radiate of Claudius II, 268–70AD, posthumous type with alter rev. Wt: 0.61g. (BM).
SF 403. Context 298 at 210/531.

76. **Allectus, 293–6** AD, **irregular quinarius.** Found in 1980 on the surface near the area of the hoard. Identified by Tony Gregory. (PRIV).
SF 66. Found in 1980 near area of hoard.

77. **House of Constantine.** Details uncertain. Found in 1980 on the surface near the area of the hoard. Identified by Tony Gregory. (PRIV).
SF 65. Found in 1980 near area of hoard.

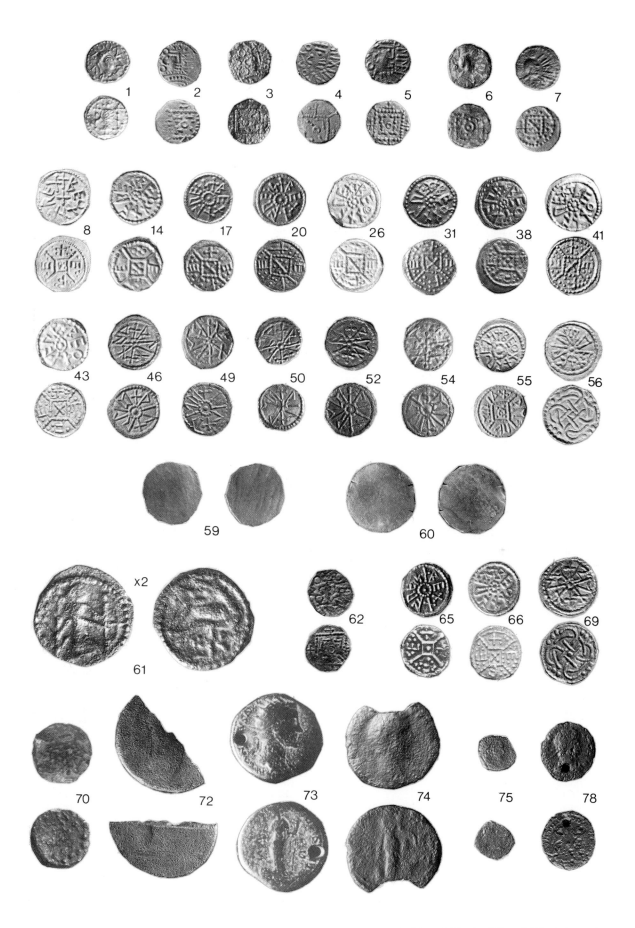

Plate XIII Coins from the Middle Harling hoard: sceattas (1–7), Beonna (8–56) and blanks (59 and 60). Other coins found at Middle Harling: Anglo-Saxon (61–78), Celtic contemporary forgery (70) and Roman (72–78).

49

78. **Constans, 337–50** AD. AE3. Rev.: two victories, Trier mint (RIC 188), holed. Wt: 1.38g. (BM).
SF 592. Filling of post-hole 827, south wall of Building B.

The archaeological context of these Roman coins suggests that they were last deposited in Anglo-Saxon times. Several of them have been subject to deliberate secondary treatment. The holed coins had been used as pendants at an intermediate stage, but their association with the mutilated pieces suggests that immediately before their final deposition they were regarded as scrap for use in decorative metalwork, or for alloying silver. Such an explanation is supported by the discovery on the site (unfortunately in an unstratified context) of small globules of base metal, evidence of small-scale metal-working in the area. Another possible role for these cut-down Roman coins is as weights, but the Middle Harling pieces lack any unit markings, and do not appear to fit any known contemporary weight system.

English

It is significant to note how many of the later Anglo-Saxon coins were struck at East Anglian mints, in particular at Norwich, confirming that currency was biased in favour of locally-issued money, suggesting a relatively limited amount of contact with places further afield.

The date of issue of the coins struck after 1180 provides only a *terminus post quem* for their deposition: Short Cross coins could have circulated until 1247, Long Cross until 1279, or a few years later; coins struck after 1279 often remained in circulation for long periods.

It is not always possible to give North and other reference numbers to coins in too poor condition for them to be attributed to a sub-type.

79. **Berhtwulf of Mercia, 840–52.** Penny, Group IA, *c.* 843–8, probably Canterbury mint, moneyer Oswulf.
Obv.: (+BER)HTVLF REX Bust type A.
Rev.: +O(SVL)F MONETA (N and E ligulate).
Wt: 0.78g, very chipped. (North 1980, 406). (PRIV).
SF 704. Found in 1980 south of Church Clump.

80. **Alfred of Wessex, 871–99.** Fragment of a penny of Two Line type, moneyer Tilwine (of London, although this type of coin does not bear the name of the mint), struck towards the end of the reign.
Obv: XE(L FR ED) RE.
Rev: (TILE)/VVNE (lest two letters ligulate).
Wt: 0.35g. Ref.: *cf* BMC Nos 374–6 (different dies). (North 1980, 636). (PRIV).
SF 100. Found in 1980 near Church Clump.

81. **St Edmund Memorial.** Penny, Post-Cuerdale group with blundered inscriptions.
Obv: CEC
Rev: +ERDNVI
Wt: 1.03g. Diameter: 17mm (North 1980, 483).
The blundered moneyer's name may be based on that of Egremond (BMC 391). This coin belongs to the extensive series of St Edmund coins with illiterate legends on small flans which were largely excluded from the Cuerdale hoard and so are mostly just later than *c.* 905 in date. (PRIV).
SF 648. Found in 1985 at TL 8799 8509.

82. **Edmund, 939–46.** Penny of Bust Crowned type, Norwich mint, moneyer Hrodgar.
Obv: +EDMVND REX (V is an inverted A).
Rev: +NRODEAR NO NORVC (N for H, E for G, first N for M).
Wt: 1.42g, chipped. (North 1980, 698). Different dies from the two known coins BMS 477–8. (PRIV).
SF 651. Found in 1986 at TL 9806 8500.

83. **Edgar, 959–75.** Cut-halfpenny (in fragments) of Bust Crowned type of East Anglian style, Norwich mint, moneyer uncertain.
Obv: (+EA)DGAR REX.
Rev: +(—)MONETA H.
Wt: 0.72g. (North 1980, 751). Dies not found in British Museum or *Syllogies*. The moneyers known in this style are Boge and Brunninc. (PRIV).

SF 89. Found in 1981 at TL 9794 8514.

84. **Aethelred II, 978–1016.** Fragment, less than a quarter of a penny of Last Small Cross type, Norwich mint, moneyer uncertain, *c.* 1009–16.
Obv: (—)LRE(—).
Rev: (—)ORD(—).
Wt: 0.23g. (North 1980, 777). (PRIV).
SF 71. Found in 1980 near area of hoard.

85. **Cnut, 1016–35.** Penny, Quatrefoil type, Norwich, moneyer Mana, *c.* 1018–24.
Obv: +CNVT REX ANGLORVI.
Rev: +MANA ONORDP.
Wt: not recorded (photograph only examined). (PRIV). Found in 1987 by Mr D. Bailey in West Harling at TL 9771 8507 (site 24454).

86. **Edward the Confessor, 1042–66.** Penny (in two pieces, broken along the line where it had been bent double) of Sovereign type, Norwich mint, moneyer Leofric, *c.* 1056–9.
Obv: EADPAR (—).
Rev: +LEOFR(IC:ON)NORDP.
The moneyer was not previously recorded in this type at Norwich, although he was known earlier and later.
Wt: 1.02g. (North 1980, 827). (PRIV).
SF 90. Found in 1981 at TL 9788 8500.

87. **Edward the Confessor, 1042–66.** Cut-farthing of Pyramids type, Oxford mint, moneyer uncertain. (North 1980, 381).
Wt: 0.20g. (BM).
SF 216. Topsoil in excavation at 210/520.

88. **Uncertain fragment.** This is a very corroded fragment of about a quarter (but not a cut-quarter) of a silver coin, possibly a late Anglo-Saxon penny.
Wt: 0.37g. (BM).
SF 236. Topsoil in excavation at 202/544.

89. **William I, 1066–87.** Tiny fragment of a penny. The only feature certainly visible is a very small head, full face. The scale and style is that of the faces on the pennies of William I's middle period. The type is possibly BMC II, as the face seems low relative to the one piece of the edge which survives, but it is not possible to be certain.
Wt: 0.15g. (PRIV).
SF 673. Found in 1986 by Mr D. Bailey in field north of excavation.

90. **Henry I, 1100–35.** Cut-farthing, BMC I, uncertain mint, moneyer, Win(—) 1100–*c.* 1102.
Obv: (+)HNR (—) (N and R ligulate).
Rev: +PIN (—-).
Wt: 0.27g. (North I, 856). A die identity has not been found for either obverse or reverse. The moneyers known to have been working around this time whose names begin with Win are Winraed of Lewes and Winedi of Canterbury; the latter is not yet recorded in this type, but is known both earlier and later. The record of the earlier issues of Henry I is however very incomplete, and it is possible that there is another, as yet unrecorded, moneyer involved. (PRIV).
SF 665. Found in 1986 by Mr D. Bailey in field north of excavation.

91. **Henry I, 1100–35.** Penny of BMC type XI, Winchester mint, moneyer Saiet, dated in North *c.* 1122–4, but by the author, *c.* 1109–10. The dating of the types of Henry I is the subject of much current discussion — see SNC Sept. 1990, 232–6, and the other chronologies cited therein.)
Obv: (H)EN/R (—).
Rev: outer legened +S(AI)T,; inner legend +PINCEST.
Wt: 1.34g. (North 1980, 867). The obverse die was also used by another Winchester moneyer, Ailwine, on a coin from the Llanthrythyd hoard in the National Museum of Wales. Saiet was not previously recorded in this type, although he was known in earlier and later types. (PRIV).
SF 621. Found in 1983 at TL 9786 8500.

92. **Henry II, 1154–89.** Short Cross cut-halfpenny class I(c?), London, moneyer uncertain, late 1180s. (North 1980, 96).
Wt: 0.59g. (PRIV).
SF 658. Found in 1986 by Mr D. Bailey in field north of excavation.

93. **John, 1199–1216.** Short Cross cut-halfpenny class Vc, Canterbury mint, moneyer Roberd, *c.* 1210. (North 1980, 971).
Wt: 0.47g. (BM).
SF 201. Topsoil in excavation at 233/521.

94. **Henry III, 1216–72.** Short Cross cut-halfpenny class VII, London, moneyer Elis, 1217–42.
Wt: 0.66g. (PRIV). SF 657. Found in 1986 by Mr D. Bailey in field north of excavation.

95. **Henry III, 1216–72.** Long Cross cut-halfpenny of class III, Lincoln, moneyer Ricard?, 1248–50.
Wt: 0.63g. (PRIV).

Plate XIV Isolated coin-finds from the Middle Harling site: Anglo-Saxon (79–88); Norman (91); later English
(92–111); German jetton (115); contemporary forgery of Cnut (118) and Kufic (120).

51

SF 654. Found in 1986 by Mr D. Bailey in field north of excavation.

96. **Henry III, 1216–72.** Cut-halfpenny of Long Cross class IIIb. Canterbury mint, moneyer Nicole, 1248–50. (North 1980, 987).
Wt: 0.53g. (PRIV).
SF 616. Found in 1983, field north of excavation.

97. **Henry III, 1216–72.** Cut-halfpenny of Long Cross class IIIb, London mint, moneyer Nicole, 1248–50. (North 1980, 987).
Wt: 0.55g. (BM).
SF 418. Context 341 at 223/526.

98. **Henry III, 1216–72.** Cut-farthing of Long Cross class IIIb, uncertain mint, moneyer Nicole, 1248–50. (North 1980, 987).
Wt: 0.32g. (BM).
SF 342. Context 153 at 203/539.

99. **Henry III, 1216–72.** Long Cross cut-farthing class Vg, London or Canterbury, moneyer Ricard, *c.* 1270. (North 1980, 997).
Wt: 0.23g. (PRIV).
SF 659. Found in 1986 by Mr D. Bailey in field north of excavation.

100. **Henry III, 1216–72.** Cut-halfpenny of Long Cross type, details uncertain, after 1247.
Wt: 0.32g. (PRIV).
SF 617. Found in field north of excavation.

101. **Edward I, 1272–1307.** Farthing, class IIIc, Lincoln mint, 1280. (North 1975, 1045). (BM).
SF 231. Topsoil in excavation at 203/522.

102. **Edward I or II.** Fragment of a penny.
Wt: 0.19g. (PRIV).
SF 692. Found in 1986 by Mr. D. Bailey in field north of excavation.

103. **Edward II, 1307–27.** Penny, class X (late), *c.* 1307–10.
Wt: 1.29g (North 1975, 'Xd', 1041). (PRIV).
SF 679. Found in 1986 by Mr D. Bailey in field north of excavation.

104. **Edward II, 1307–27.** Penny, class X (late), *c.* 1307–10. Canterbury mint. Very worn and clipped, suggesting deposition in the early 15th century.
Wt: 0.97g. (PRIV).
SF 618. Found in field north of excavation.

105. **Edward III, 1327–77.** Penny of the Pre-Treaty Coinage, 1351–61, Durham mint. Very worn and clipped, suggesting deposition in the early 15th century.
Wt: 0.50g. (PRIV).
SF 619. Found in field north of excavation.

106. **Edward III, 1327–77.** Halfpenny, Florin Coinage, 1344–51, London. (North 1975, 1132).
Wt: 0.57g. (PRIV).
SF 656. Found in 1986 by Mr D. Bailey in field north of excavation.

107. **Henry VI, First Reign, 1422–61.** Halfpenny of the Leaf Pellet Issue, 1445–54. (North 1975, 1512).
Wt: 0.38g. (BM).
SF 273. Topsoil in excavation at 230/532.

108. **Currency forgery copying a penny of Edward IV, 1461–70 and 1471–83.** Reverse of York type with a quatrefoil in the centre, but with a London inscription.
Wt: 0.43g. (BM).
SF 378. Context 216 at 218/526.

109. **Elizabeth I, 1558–1603.** Half-groat i.m. crescent, 1587–90 (North 1975, 2016).
Wt: 0.99g. (PRIV).
SF 671. Found in 1986 by Mr D. Bailey in field north of excavation.

110. **Elizabeth I, 1558–1603.** Threepence, 1566. Coin identified by Sue Margeson; weight not recorded. (PRIV).
SF 10. Topsoil, area of 1981 excavation.

111. **Elizabeth I, 1558–1603.** Penny, initial mark castle, London mint. (North 1975, 2001).
Wt: 0.48g. (BM).
SF 435. Context *446* at 229/540.

This group of isolated site finds shows that after its early period abnormally rich in coins, the Middle Harling pattern of coin-finds becomes typical of many other sites. The wealthy 8th-century phase is followed by a fairly rich later Anglo-Saxon phase where coins are still more plentiful than is usual in a coin-list of this scale. Thereafter, there is the predictable odd Norman coin, followed, typically, by more plentiful finds from the 13th century, although the Short Cross period is rather under-represented. The latest pieces are from the mid-16th century. The absence of the very common early 17th-century token farthings, and the private tokens current later in the 17th century, suggest that the site was no longer occupied, at least for purposes involving the regular use of coin. The high proportion of cut coins and other low denominations is typical of site finds; in hoards, the lower denominations are discriminated against, where possible, in favour of coins of higher individual value.

Tokens and Jettons

112. **17th-century farthing token of Norwich City, 1668 (holed).**
Wt: 3.38g. Ref.: Williamson 1967, 226. (PRIV).
SF 678. Found in 1986 by Mr D. Bailey in field north of excavation.

113. **Sterling jetton,** period of Edward II, 1307–27, rosette within tressure/a rosette in each angle of a cross. (Berry 7/-).
Wt: 0.86g. (PRIV). SF 620. Found in field north of excavation.

114. **Fragment of a French 15th-century jetton.** All that is visible on one side is G followed by an upright which is possibly a part of an R *i.e.* part of the common legend AVE MARIA GRACIA PLENA(or variant).
Wt: 0.28g. (PRIV).
SF 694. Found in 1986 by Mr D. Bailey in field north of excavation.

115. **Nuremberg jetton,** Ship type, 16th century, holed.
Wt: 1.57g. Diameter 28mm. (BM).
SF 258. Topsoil in excavation at 223/525.

116. **Nuremberg jetton,** Hans Krauwinckel, *fl.* 1580–1610.
Obv: Reichsapfel, GOTES SEGEN MACHT REICH.
Rev: Three crowns and three lis around rosette, HANNS KRAVWINCKEL IN NVR.
Wt: 0.72g. Diameter 21 mm. (PRIV).
SF 687. Found in 1986 by Mr D. Bailey in field north of excavation.

Scottish

117. **William I, 1165–1214.** Cut-halfpenny, Short Cross type, 3rd Coinage, Posthumous issue; moneyers Hue and Walter.
Wt: 0.66g. *cf.* Stewart (1967) No.20. (PRIV).
SF 688. Found in 1986 by Mr D. Bailey in field north of excavation.

Contemporary Imitation

118. **Imitation of penny of Cnut, Short Cross type** (BMC XVI) copied from a coin of Chester mint by the moneyer Leofsige.
Obv: CNVT followed by a blundered REX, all retrograde. Bust also retrograde (*ie* facing to right, rather than normally to left).
Rev: +LEOFSIGE ON LEII (retrograde).
Wt: 0.87g (bent).
Both sides of this coin are retrograde, and it is not of official English style. The weight is on the low side, compared with official coins. The style is similar to that of Scandinavian imitations, although neither die has so far been linked into the known chains of undoubtedly Scandinavian coins. The absence of 'pecking', so regularly found on coins of this period which circulated in Scandinavia, suggests that this could be an English imitation, rather than a Scandinavian one. The coin is bent, but it is difficult to decide whether this is deliberate (as coins often are from Viking Age contexts in Scandinavia) or merely accidental. Its true status must for the moment remain open. (PRIV). Found in 1983 by Mr J. Rich in West Harling at TL 9778 8495 (site 19762).

European

119. **Duchy of Brabant.** John I, 1261–92, cut-quarter of a Lion sterling.
Obv: E + (D/VX BRA/BANT)I (or variant) Lion of Brabant in shield.
Rev: (XID/EIG/RAT)IA+ Long cross voided, (W/A/L)/T in angles.
Wt: 0.32g.
Lion sterlings are less often found in England than other Continental issues closer in their designs to English pennies, but cut quarters no doubt escaped detection more easily in circulation than full coins. Chautard (1871) No.89. (PRIV).
SF 689. Found in 1986 by Mr D. Bailey in field north of excavation.

Kufic

120. **Imitation of a Samanid silver dirhem of Isma'il b. Ahmad, 892–907AD,** with the name of the Caliph al-Mu'tadid in the area, and that of his predecessor al-Mu'tamid in the margin. The inscriptions are partly retrograde. This coin belongs to a group of imitations dated by G. Rispling to *c.* 893–902AD. Weight not recorded. (Identified by the late Mr N.M. Lowick, British Museum). (PRIV).

SF 647. Found in 1985 at TL 9802 8505.

Kufic dirhams and their copies occur in several British hoards of the Viking period, and an increasing number of single finds of such coins are being recorded, especially from East Anglia; a Viking-Age forgery of a dirhem was found at York (Hall 1984, 92). The evidence is overwhelming that such coins travelled westwards from the Caliphate to England via the Viking trade routes through Russia, the Baltic and Scandinavia.

III. The Non-ferrous Metal Objects
by Sue Margeson

The artefacts discussed here were recovered both by metal-detecting of the ploughed surface and by excavation. They are characterised by a wide date range, though the report focuses mainly on the Saxon period.

A number of finds made since 1986 has been recorded for the Norfolk SMR. These include another fragment of the repoussé strip (SF 702, *cf.* 88–93), a medieval belt-fitting with decorated buckle and oval suspension loop, from which are suspended two pierced heads of broken keys? or toilet articles (SF 706), and a gilded copper alloy medieval buckle and plate (SF 701). There is also a tongue-shaped strap-end (with repaired split end), the surface of which is divided into two by a central longitudinal rib (SF 713, south-west of Church Clump).

This type is apparently Anglo-Scandinavian and 10th century (pers. comm. J. Graham-Campbell). Several have now been recorded in Norfolk (*cf.* Bawsey site 12364, SF 79). All catalogue entries are copper alloy unless otherwise stated. Each entry is given its small find (SF) number. This is followed by the initials of the finder of those objects not recovered in the excavation: (T.F.) Tony Frost, (D.B.) David Bailey. The context number follows, although context *100*, for topsoil finds in the excavation, is omitted. A context description is then given, except in the case of objects found in spits in the brown soil. Finally the co-ordinates, to the nearest square metre, are entered, *e.g.* 233/525.

The stray-finds (non-ferrous metals Nos 1–3, 8, 9, 11, 13–15, 19, 20, 26–29, 31, 32, 40, 42, 43, 47, 49, 54, 55, 58, 59–64, 68–70, 72, 74, 78, 79, 84, 96, 103, 120, 132; iron No. 115) are in Norwich Castle Museum; the few remaining stray-finds are still in private possession. The excavation finds are in the British Museum.

Brooches
(Fig. 34)

The head-plate of a small-long brooch, of 6th century date, has unusual incised cross-hatching (1). The 10th-century Viking-period trefoil brooch (2) with stylised leaf

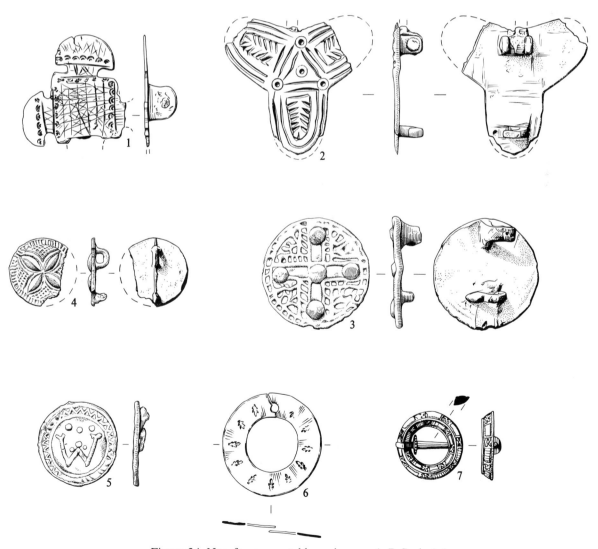

Figure 34 Non-ferrous metal brooches nos 1–7. Scale 1:1.

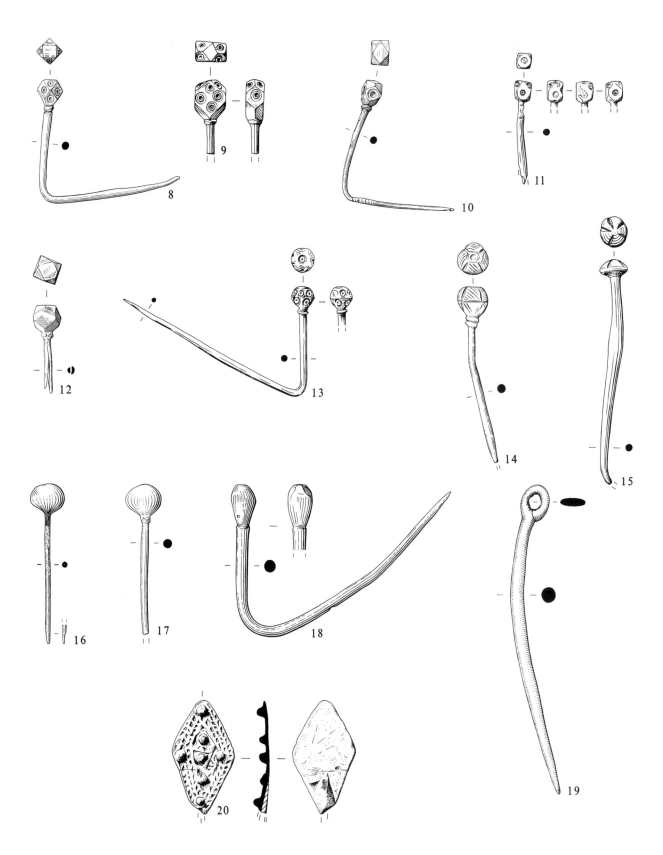

Figure 35 Non-ferrous metal pins nos 8–20. Scale 1:1.

ornament is of a type known from Hedeby (Capelle 1968, pl. 4, nos 3 and 4). The leaf ornament derives ultimately from Frankish plant ornament, and is probably a stylised version of a single acanthus leaf. Several similar copper alloy trefoil brooches have been found in Norfolk and Suffolk (Margeson 1982, 208–210, pl. IV), one from Bircham (now in King's Lynn Museum 225.980), and one from Carlton Colville, Suffolk (in private possession). These bear stylised leaf ornament which is closely related to the Harling example. Trefoil brooches were used in the late 9th and early 10th centuries to pin the shawl together, and were usually worn in Scandinavia with pairs of oval brooches. The fashion for trefoil brooches was popular in the Danelaw, and they may have been worn as alternatives to disc brooches.

The 10th-century lead disc brooch (3) with cast decoration is a crude imitation of the elaborate silver disc brooches with studs and bosses, and may be compared with one from Mildenhall, now in the British Museum (Wilson 1964, cat. no. 54) and one from Thetford now in Norwich Castle Museum (Goodall, A.R. 1984, fig. 109, no. 1).

The pewter disc brooch with a quatrefoil motif within a ribbed border (4) may also be 10th century in date. The form of the lug and catchplate and the ribbed decoration have particular similarities with those on No. 3.

The lead disc decorated with cast ornament in the form of a 'W' within a chevron border is medieval. The damaged fittings on the reverse suggest it was a brooch, or more likely a badge (possibly a pilgrim badge, with loops for attachment). If it is a pilgrim badge, the 'W' may signify Walsingham.

The medieval ring brooch (6) of flat section, with a hole through which the pin was secured, is decorated with stamped leaf motifs. It is 13th or 14th century.

The fine gilded ring brooch (7) with engraved ornament is 14th century. The pin with decorated collar is seated on a narrow bar, a characteristic of 14th-century brooches. The decoration of alternating rosettes and rectangular fields is also known from other 14th-century jewellery such as finger-rings.

1. **Small-long brooch head-plate fragment** with crescent stamps, scored roughly with cross-hatching.
   SF 622 (T.F.). West-south-west of the excavation at TL 9785 8509.
2. **Trefoil brooch fragment** with stylised leaf ornament and stamped ring-and-dots at the junctions of the arms and in the centre. H-shaped lug, and catchplate on reverse; traces of iron pin in lug.
   SF 59 (T.F.). South of Church Clump.
3. **Lead disc brooch,** with cast cruciform decoration with a boss at the end of each arm and in the centre; quadrants decorated with stylised ?interlace. Ribbed border. Metal not analysed.
   SF 60 (T.F.). East-south-east of Church Clump.
4. **Pewter disc brooch,** with cast quatrefoil in centre, cross-hatching in spandrels, and ribbed border. Remains of lug and catchplate on reverse; casting seam on reverse. Metal analysed in BM.
   SF 225. Topsoil in excavation at 228/529.
5. **Lead disc** with cast chevron border; 'W' in centre. (?)Lug or loop traces on reverse. ?Brooch or badge. Metal analysed in BM.
   SF 281. Topsoil in excavation at 226/538.
6. **Ring brooch** with stamped leaf motifs; hole for attachment of pin.
   SF 644 (T.F.). South of Church Clump.
7. **Gilded ring brooch** decorated with alternating panels and quatrefoils; bevelled. Pin with moulded discoidal collar which has nicked edges; pin attached over narrow bar.
   SF 95 (T.F.). TL 9805 8522.

Pins
(Figs 35 and 36)

Pins with decorated heads, often having collared shafts, and sometimes with mid-stem swellings, are known from many Middle Saxon sites (Whitby (Peers and Radford 1943); Brandon, Suffolk, and others). 1–18 are of characteristic types, with faceted heads decorated with ring-and-dots, or heads of different shapes decorated in other ways.

The pin with looped head may be a brooch pin (19). The decoration on the lozenge-shaped (?)pin-head (20) is reminiscent of the ornament on the lead disc brooch (3), and the object may be of similar date.

The decorated spherical pin-head (21) is of a type well known in 8th- and 9th-century contexts, with the filigree wire forming spirals on the surface (cf. the pin from Wicken Bonhunt, Essex in Musty, Wade and Rogerson 1973, 287, and two unpublished examples from Brandon, Suffolk).

8. **Collared shaft,** faceted head decorated with stamped ring-and-dots.
   SF 75 (T.F.). North-east of Church Clump.
9. Fragment with **collared shaft,** faceted head decorated with stamped ring-and-dots.
   SF 94 (T.F.). TL 9798 8511.
10. **Collared shaft,** faceted head decorated with stamped ring-and-dots. Zone of transverse incised lines at mid-stem may have prevented pin from slipping.
    SF 240. Topsoil in excavation at 212/517.
11. Fragment with **faceted head** decorated with stamped ring-and-dots.
    SF 643 (T.F.). South of Church Clump.
12. **Collared shaft,** faceted head; shaft split, faulty casting?
    SF 255. Topsoil in excavation at 200/525.
13. **Collared shaft,** biconical head decorated with stamped ring-and-dots.
    SF 623 (T.F.). TL 9802 8510.
14. **Collared shaft,** biconical head decorated with roughly engraved lines. Point missing.
    SF 67 (T.F.). Topsoil in area of excavation.
15. **Hemispherical head** decorated with five engraved lines radiating from centre. Mid-shaft swelling. Point missing.
    SF 650 (T.F.). South of Church Clump.
16. **Globular head;** point tapers asymmetrically.
    SF 227. Topsoil in excavation at 2241/532.
17. Fragment with **collared shaft,** globular head.
    SF 304. Context *105* at 226/514.
18. **Elongated head.**
    SF 238. Topsoil in excavation at 210/544.
19. **Looped head.**
    SF 76 (T.F.). North-east of Church Clump.
20. Lead **lozenge-shaped pin-head,** with three diagonal bands of cast ribbed ornament, and seven symmetrical bosses. Reverse has socketed projection into which an iron shaft was presumably inserted (traces of iron in socket).
    SF 97 (T.F.). TL 9790 8511.
21. Gilded **spherical pin-head,** decorated with filigree wire forming spirals on each hemisphere with a median band of filigree. Granule in centre of each spiral. Hollow shaft fragment has filigree collar at top.
    SF 400. Context *275* at 210/534.

Figure 36 Non-ferrous metal pin-head no. 21. Scale 1:1.

Pendant
(Fig. 37)

22. Gilded fish pendant. Uncertain date, probably modern.
SF 703 (T.F.). TL 9806 8521.

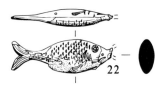

Figure 37 Non-ferrous metal pendant no. 22 . Scale 1:1.

Finger-rings
(Fig. 38)

Finger-rings with tapering terminals twisted together are known from Late Saxon contexts at Thetford (Goodall, A.R. 1984, fig. 110, nos 12 and 13). These examples (23 and 24) are decorated with stamped annulets (23) and ribbing (24). Another tiny example has overlapping terminals and is decorated with ring-and-dots (25; possibly a child's or a decorative binding ring). Undecorated finger-rings with overlapping terminals (26–32) are also known from Late Saxon contexts at Thetford (Goodall, A.R. 1984, fig. 110, nos 17, 19–21).

The silver-gilt finger-ring (33) is a well known type, with the bezel in the form of clasped hands, and a religious inscription. It may be compared with a similar finger-ring in the Castle Museum, Norwich (76.94 (45)), and a group of silver and silver-gilt 15th-century rings illustrated by Oman (Oman 1974, pl. 54, A–E).

The unusual finger-ring (34) with the flattened ends of the loop overlapping to form the bezel is probably medieval.

23. **Finger-ring** with tapering terminals which are twisted together; decorated with unevenly spaced stamped annulets.
SF 572. Context *778,* spit at 232/531.
24. **Finger-ring** with tapering terminals twisted together; decorated with two longitudinal and sunken zones of stamped 'ribbing'.
SF 285. Topsoil in excavation at 226/540.
25. (?)**Finger-ring** made of strip with tapering, overlapping terminals with ends broken; decorated with stamped ring-and-dots.
SF 259. Topsoil in excavation at 227/522.
26– **Finger-rings**, penannular, with tapering overlapping terminals.
32. SFs 61, 69, 77, 98 (T.F.). North of Church Clump; topsoil in area of excavation; north-east of Church Clump; TL 9803 8507.
SF 363. Context *188,* filling of Post-medieval bone-pit *154.*
SFs 624, 639 (T.F.). TL 9796 8517; south of Church Clump.
33. **Silver-gilt finger-ring** with bezel in form of clasped hands; Lombardic inscription: IHC NAZARENS R. Shoulders decorated with zones of engraved crosses.
Site 21025, SF 4. East end of field north-west of excavation (D.B.).
34. **Finger-ring** with bezel formed of two overlapping semi-circular plates, surface rough (applied decoration missing). Shoulders decorated.
SF 528. Context *571,* filling of medieval feature *645,* 223/514.

Hooked Tags
(Fig. 39)

Hooked tags (Graham-Campbell 1982, 148 advocates the use of the term hooked tag) occur in three basic types, circular, triangular or lobed, and seem to have been used from the 9th to the 11th centuries for a variety of purposes associated with dress and accessories.

The silver tags from Tetney were probably used to fasten a purse as they were found with a coin hoard deposited before AD 970 (Wilson 1964, cat. nos 86 and 87; Graham-Campbell 1982, note 30). The tags from Winchester may have fastened garters, found as they were

beneath the knees of a skeleton on Cathedral Green (Wilson 1965, 262–264).

The circular hooked tags (35–39) are perhaps the most common. Those decorated with ring-and-dot may be compared with examples from 11th-century contexts on many sites, including Thetford (Goodall, A.R. 1984, fig. 111, 32 and 33).

Triangular hooked tags are known with elaborate ornament, such as the fine silver pair from Winchester of 9th-century date with Trewhiddle-style decoration. Simpler 10th-century examples are also known, such as one made of copper alloy from the Castle bailey site, Norwich (Margeson and Williams 1985, fig. 24, no. 5). The triangular hooked tag with an unusual stamped border of tiny ring-and-dots (40) is probably also 10th century. Triangular hooked tags with simpler decoration or no decoration at all (41–44) could date from the 9th or 10th century. The undecorated triangular tags from Tetney provide the closest parallels (Wilson 1964, cat. nos 86, 87).

The lobed hooked tags also range from elaborate silver examples decorated with Trewhiddle ornament (Green 1980, 351–353 and Graham-Campbell 1982), to simpler ones decorated with ring-and-dots (45, 46) which are probably 10th or 11th century. Those decorated with engraved linear or geometric motifs are probably also 10th or 11th century (47, 48). The style of the engraving is typical of the Late Saxon period.

Hooked tags were also known in the early post-medieval period (16th, 17th centuries). These have rectangular or circular loops for attachment. A related type is the example from Harling (49) with a central sunken circular field, perhaps once inlaid, further decorated with diagonal hatching around it. However, instead of a loop for attachment, there is a short spike in the same plane as the body of the tag. The tag may be purely decorative, and may simply have dangled from a belt or garment, hooked into the leather or fabric. Other similar tags have been recorded for the Sites and Monuments Record (such as one from Weeting-with-Broomhill, Co. No. 25523).

35. **Circular**, with ring-and-dots; two attachment holes.
SF 25 (T.F.). Topsoil in 1981 trench.
36. **Circular**, with ring-and-dots; two attachment holes.
SF 249. Topsoil in excavation at 232/514.
37. **Circular**, decorated both front and back with ring-and-dots; two attachment holes.
SF 464. Context *447,* at 223/506.
38. **Circular**, two attachment holes.
SF 636 (T.F.). Field north of excavation.
39. **Circular**, white-metal-coated; two attachment holes.
SF 84 (T.F.). TL 9801 8507.
40. **Triangular**, decorated with rows of stamped annulets between ribbed borders; two attachment holes.
SF 70 (T.F.). Topsoil in area of excavation.
41. **Triangular**, decorated with two punches circles below single attachment hole.
SF 320. Context *124,* filling of medieval ditch *604,* at 233/524.
42. **Triangular**, decorated with repoussé boss in centre; two attachment holes.
SF 641 (T.F.). South of Church Clump.
43. **Triangular**, hook missing; incised double-contoured border.
SF 92 (T.F.). TL 9803 8519.
44. **Triangular** with one attachment hole.
SF 414. Context *341* at 217/530.
45. **Decorated** with ring-and-dots; with two lobes pierced for attachment.
SF 509. Context *114,* filling of medieval ditch *138* at 229/519.
46. **Decorated** with ring-and-dots and engraved lines; two lobes pierced for attachment.
SF 664 (D.B.). Field north of excavation.
47. **Decorated** with engraved symmetrical motif; two lobes pierced for attachment.

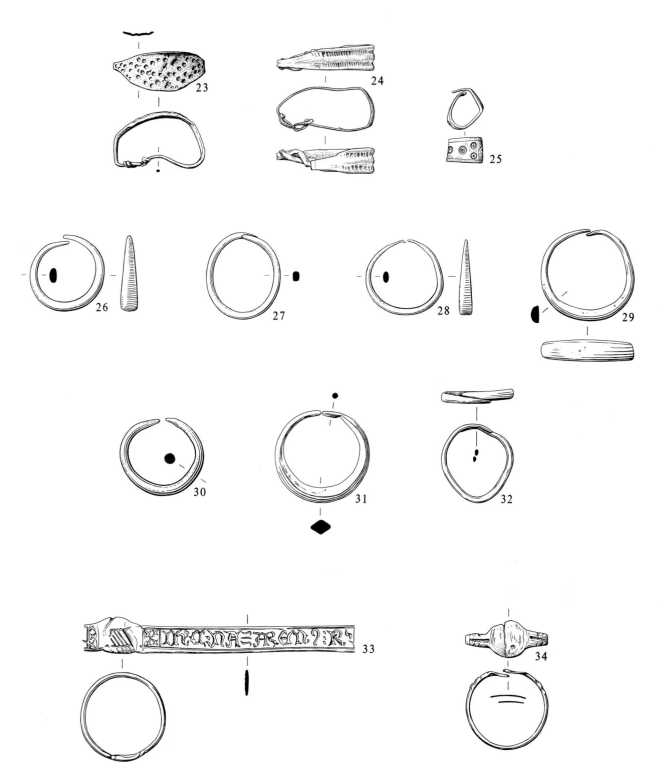

Figure 38 Non-ferrous metal finger-rings nos 23–34. Scale 1:1

SF 646 (T.F.). 12m east of south-east corner of excavation.
48. **Decorated** with engraved cruciform motif; three lobes pierced for attachment.
    SF 517. Context *517,* upper filling of medieval pit *589* at 230/524.
49. **Circular** with central sunken field once inlaid (?). Traces of diagonal hatching around. Spike at one side, hook at other.
    SF 99 (T.F.). TL 9785 8511.

Buttons
(Fig. 39)
These are probably 16th or 17th century.

50. Gilded, with integral loop.

SF 10a (T.F.). Topsoil in 1981 trench.
51. Gilded with integral loop.
    SF 276. Topsoil in excavation at 210/531.

Buckles and Belt-Fittings
(Fig. 40)
The D-shaped buckle with pairs of engraved lines and shaped tongue-rest is Early Saxon (52). The buckles with engraved linear ornament on moulded loops are 13th century (53–55). The buckle with expanded loop, and ring-and-dot decoration may be compared with one

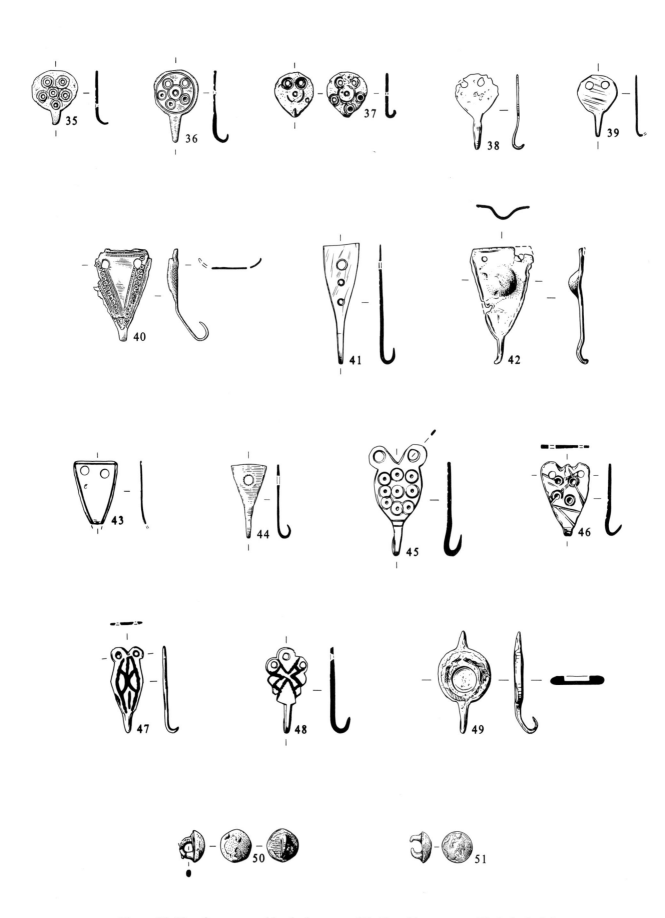

Figure 39 Non-ferrous metal hooked tags nos 35–49 and buttons nos 50–1. Scale 1:1.

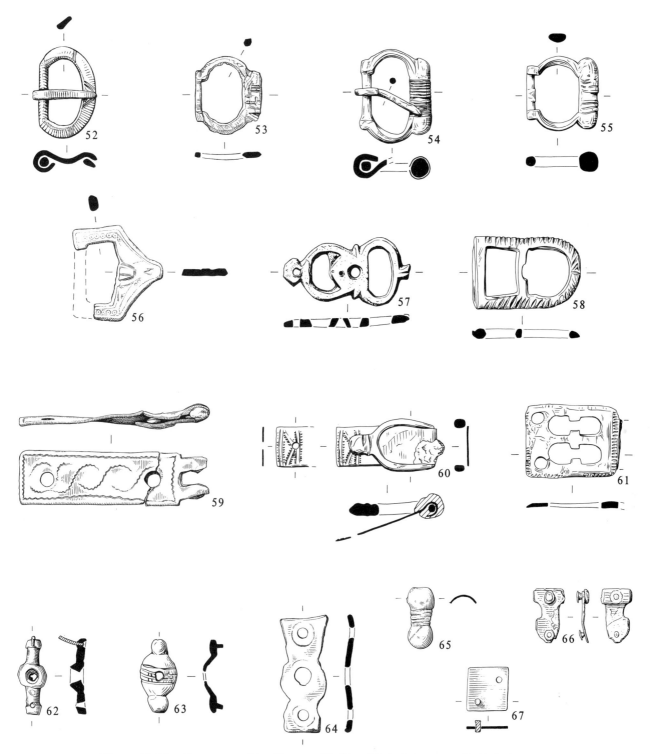

Figure 40 Non-ferrous metal buckles nos 52–61 and belt-fittings nos 62–7. Scale 1:1.

excavated on the Castle bailey site, Norwich (Margeson and Williams 1985, fig. 24, no. 7), and two from 13th-century contexts at Riseholme, Lincolnshire (Thompson 1960, fig. 34, no. 2), and King's Lynn (Clarke and Carter 1977, fig. 130, no. 14).

The elaborate asymmetric double-looped buckle (57) is late 14th century. The smaller loop with lobed terminal must be decorative, because of the width of the moulded central part of the frame. The buckle would function in a similar way to those with integral plates, a well-known 14th-century type, such as two from London (cf. LMMC pl. LXXVII, nos 15, 16). The large central hole is for the

buckle pin, and the smaller holes in the centre and in the lobed terminal are for attachment to the belt. The double-looped buckle with ribbed decoration (58), and the gilded buckle-plate (59) with engraved ornament are late medieval.

The stirrup-shaped hasp with its decorated attachment plate (60) is well known from excavations, and stray finds, though its precise function is uncertain. It is most likely a belt-fastener.

The openwork buckle-plate (61) with key-hole-shaped openings may be compared with one excavated in Lund from a context of 1150–1200 (Mårtensson 1976, fig. 272).

Belt-stiffeners like 62 and 63 are of 13th-century date, and some survive *in situ* on belts (Fingerlin 1971, cat. no. 545).

Later medieval belt-stiffeners are rectangular or lobed, and often gilded (64), or double-lobed with transverse ribbing in the centre (65).

52. **D-shaped** with engraved lines on tongue-rest and corners of frame.
SF 357. Context *173* filling of post-medieval ditch *854* at 206/544.
53. **D-shaped** with moulded frame with engraved lines.
SF 326. Context *153*, at 209/526.
54. **D-shaped** with moulded ribbed frame.
SF 630 (T.F.). Field north of excavation.
55. **D-shaped** with moulded ribbed frame.
SF 633 (T.F.). Field north of excavation.
56. **Expanded frame**; decorated with ring-and-dots.
SF 297. Topsoil in excavation at 205/540.
57. **Oval** with integral openwork attachment plate with rivet holes and lobe terminal. Projecting tongue-rest.
SF 500. Context *450*, at 232/519.
58. **Double-looped** with engraved ribbing.
SF 632 (T.F.). Field north of excavation.
59. **Gilded buckle-plate** with engraved S-shapes within wavy border.
SF 63 (T.F.). Topsoil in area of excavation.
60. **Stirrup-shaped hasp** with decorated rectangular attachment plate.
SF 629 (T.F.). Field north of excavation.
61. **Openwork buckle-plate** with key-hole shaped openings and ribbed border.
SF 634 (T.F.). Field north of excavation.
62. **Belt-stiffener** with silver rivet.
SF 72 (T.F.). Topsoil in area of excavation.
63. **Belt-stiffener** with integral shanks at each end; central hole, decorative. Iron on reverse.
SF 101 (T.F.). Near, and probably south of, Church Clump.
64. **Gilded belt-stiffener** with three pierced holes, central one possibly only decorative.
SF 62 (T.F.). Topsoil in area of excavation.
65. **Belt-stiffener**; spikes for attachment missing.
SF 315. Context *105*, at 229/532.
66. **Belt-fitting** with reinforcement strip and two rivets with circular roves.
SF 237. Topsoil in excavation at 207/545.
67. **Belt-fitting** with two rivet-holes, one containing an iron rivet.
SF 265. Topsoil in excavation at 232/525.

Strap-ends
(Fig. 41)

The strap-ends with animal-head terminals (68–71) belong to a group of 9th-century strap ends, and may be compared with a number from Whitby Abbey (Wilson 1964, cat. nos 115–29).

The silver and copper alloy one (68) is a particularly fine example, with a pair of entwined Trewhiddle-type animals in the central field, with the characteristic speckling on the animal bodies (Wilson 1964, cat. nos 94–96; Graham-Campbell 1982, 144–151). It is most unusual in having a silver front plate riveted to a copper alloy body. The animal-head terminal is modelled in deep relief, with attention to details of ears, eyes and nostrils.

The copper alloy strap-end (69) has a single backward-facing Trewhiddle-type animal in the central field, with speckled body. The animal on 70 is also a typical Trewhiddle-style animal, with double-nicked contours. Both 69 and 70 have traces of white inlay, which may be enamel. The animal-head terminal on 70 is squared off at the muzzle, possibly a faulty casting or a break in antiquity. 71 is unusual in being completely in the form of an animal-head with lobes at the top of the ears; there is a rivet in each lobe.

72 is similar to 68–71 but has an unusual pointed terminal (compare some from Whitby Abbey, Wilson 1964, cat. nos 124–126).

73, an unusual hooked tag, is included with this group because of the animal head above the hook. Hooked tags with animal heads above the hook are known, such as an unprovenanced example in the British Museum (Webster and Backhouse 1991, cat. no. 197b).

The wedge-shaped strap-end (74) decorated with zones of transverse lines, is of a different type, made of folded sheet metal. A similar piece was amongst the Beeston Tor hoard (Wilson 1964, cat. no.4); it too is made of sheet metal doubled over, with a circular terminal in which is a single rivet. It can be dated to pre-875.

The fragment of an openwork tongue-shaped strap-end (75) is decorated with stylised foliage in a debased Winchester style, and is a well known 10th-century type (Backhouse *et al* 1984, cat. nos 82, 83).

The fragment of a possible strap-end (76) with part of an inscription is medieval.

The 'lyre-shaped' belt-chape (77) may be compared with a 14th-century example from London with a similar human figure in the centre holding a sword or staff (LMMC fig. 85, no.1). Fingerlin (1971, 162–76) dates buckles and chapes of this group from about 1360 into the 1430s or 1440s. A similar buckle from Hillington, Norfolk was mercury silvered in order to make a copper alloy buckle have the appearance of silver (Hook, La Nièce and Cherry 1988, 301–305).

68. **Silver and copper alloy strap-end** with animal-head terminal. The silver decorated front plate is riveted with four silver rivets to a copper alloy body which has a split end. The split end has one silver rivet and one copper alloy rivet, also piercing the front plate, to secure the belt. Below them is a U-shaped field containing a stylised trefoil leaf. In the central rectangular field are two back-to-back and intertwining animals with speckled bodies. The animal-head terminal is in deep relief. The surface is further decorated with inlaid niello.
SF 710 (T.F.). Near Church Clump.
69. **Strap-end with animal-head terminal.** The split end has two rivet holes. Below is a U-shaped field which contains a double inverted 'V'. The rectangular field has a backward-facing animal in profile, with a speckled body, three-toed feet, and a tail ending in a leaf. The animal-head terminal is very stylised. There are traces of inlay (?enamel).
SF 638 (T.F.). South of Church Clump.
70. **Strap-end with animal-head terminal.** The split end has two copper alloy rivets. The U-shaped field below has a double inverted 'V'. There is a ribbed border to the strap-end, and in the rectangular field, an animal with double-nicked contours. The large animal-head terminal is squared off at the base. There are traces of inlay (?enamel).
SF 93 (T.F.). TL 9789 8508.
71. **Strap-end** in form of animal head with stylised muzzle and elongated ears. Split end has two rivets in lobes at top of ears.
SF 524. Context *548*, filling of late Saxon phase of ditch *700*, at 205/528.
72. **Strap-end** with pointed terminal; divided into two longitudinal fields covered with roughly scored transverse lines, possibly to take inlay, or enamel.
SF 68 (T.F.). Topsoil in area of excavation.
73. **Hooked tag** with animal-head terminal which curves inwards to form hook, end broken; rivet hole at expanded end.
SF 301. Context *105*, at 231/507.
74. **Wedge-shaped strap-end** made of folded over strip of sheet metal with circular terminal with central rivet. Decorated with zones of transverse bands below.
SF 81 (T.F.). Field north of excavation.
75. **Tongue-shaped strap-end** with openwork decoration in the form of stylised foliage.
SF 628 (T.F.). Field north of excavation.
76. **Strap-end fragment**, inscribed 'E', one rivet.
SF 24 (T.F.). Topsoil in 1981 trench.
77. **'Lyre-shaped' belt-chape** with engraved linear ornament on the square body of the chape. The lyre-shaped part has foliate scrolls

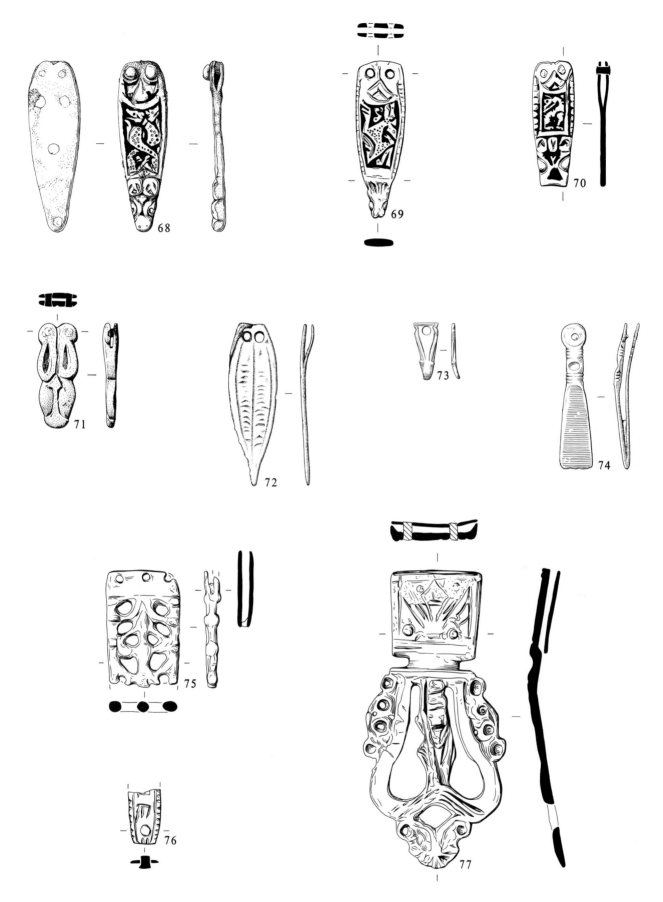

Figure 41 Non-ferrous metal strap-ends nos 68–76 and belt-chape no. 77. Scale 1:1.

on each side and a foliate terminal; in the centre is a figure with a sword or staff.
SF 627. Field north of excavation.

Chapes
(Fig. 42)
The U-shaped openwork sword chape (78) may be compared with one from London (LMMC fig. 88, no. 1), dated possibly to the 14th century. The dagger chape with solid knob terminal and decorated with stamped annulets (79) is also medieval.

78. **Sword chape fragment**, U-shaped with openwork decoration.
    SF 631 (T.F.). Field north of excavation.
79. **Dagger chape** with solid knob terminal, decorated with punched annulets.
    SF 645 (T.F.). South of Church Clump.

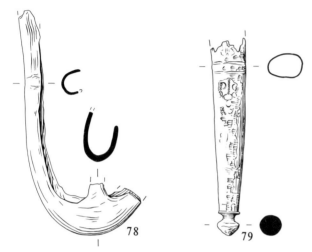

Figure 42 Non-ferrous metal chapes nos 78–9.
Scale 1:1.

Toilet Article
(Fig. 43)
The tweezers with expanded arms and decorated with ring-and-dots (80) may be compared with two pairs from North Elmham, one silver and one copper alloy (Wade-Martins 1980a, figs 262 no. 4 and 263 no. 4), and with a pair from Whitby (Peers and Radford 1943, 62, fig. 13, no. 6). These also have expanded arms with in-turned ends. The North Elmham examples come from a Period I ditch (Middle Saxon) (copper alloy), and from Period II (upper filling of a Middle Saxon ditch) (silver). The Harling tweezers are probably also Middle Saxon.

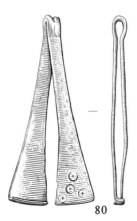

Figure 43 Non-ferrous metal tweezers no. 80. Scale 1:1.

80. **Tweezers** with expanded arms, decorated at both ends with ring-and-dots. Ribbing on bow; ends of arms turned in.
    SF 293. Topsoil in excavation at 208/519.

Seal Matrices
(Fig. 44)
There are three fine medieval seal matrices (81–83).

The silver seal matrix set with an intaglio gem-stone (81) is one of a group of 13th-century seal matrices with intaglios cut by medieval seal-cutters (Henig and Heslop 1986). It belonged to a member of the seignurial family of Middle and West Harling (see p.25).

The lead circular seal matrix (82) is a well known stock seal type of the late 12th or 13th century, with a stylised fleur-de-lis motif, and inscribed with the name of the owner. This example is of particular interest as it belonged to Michael, son of Richard of Harling.

The pointed oval copper alloy seal matrix (83) is 14th century. The pelican in her piety was often used on personal seals. It too is inscribed with the name of the owner.

John Cherry has contributed the following note:-

The silver seal matrix (81) is an interesting addition to the medieval gem-set seals already known from Norfolk. Three of these were published by Henig and Heslop (1986) and a fourth found in Diss in 1850 was in the Nelson collection in 1936 (Babelon 1902, 87–88; Demay 1877, xvi, no. 187). The jasper engraved with the equestrian figure is medieval, and not classical. It was pointed out by Babelon and Demay that such equestrian intaglios were medieval (Demay 1881, 40, no. 358). The earliest evidence on an impression for the use of medieval equestrian intaglios is on the seal of Pierre de Longueville from Normandy dated to the end of the 12th century. The closest parallel to the Harling seal is that ploughed up at Potterne in Wiltshire and now in the British Museum (Tonnochy 1952, no. 704). This is set with a similar jasper intaglio with an equestrian figure. The gem is set in the same axis as the Harling seal with the horse's head to the handle of the seal. It is dated by Tonnochy to the 13th century. Unlike the Harling seal it has the impersonal inscription + QUE: TIBI: LEGO: LEGE (Read what I send to you). The Harling seal belonged to Jeffrey de Furneaux. The surname is presumably derived from the word for a kiln or furnace. The dating of gem set seals needs further study but from the style of the lettering a date in the first half of the 13th century is most likely.

81. **Silver oval seal matrix** set with green jasper engraved with an equestrian figure. There is a loop handle projecting from the top. The legend reads + SIGILL' GALFRIDE FURNEUS. The stone is set so that the head of the horse is set towards the cross at the top of the seal.
    Dimensions: height of seal with handle 36mm
    width of seal 23mm
    length of gem 18mm
    width of gem 13cm
    SF 220. Topsoil in excavation at 224/522.
82. **Lead circular seal matrix** with loop for suspension on edge; stylised fleur-de-lis in centre.
    Legend: SIGIL' MICAELIS FILI RICARDI DE HERLING.
    SF 1 (D.B.). Site 21025 east end of field north-west of excavation.
83. **Copper alloy pointed oval seal matrix** with loop for suspension at top of reverse; pelican in her piety.
    Legend: S' THOME DE ERVDENVNIR.
    SF 626 (T.F.). Field north of excavation.

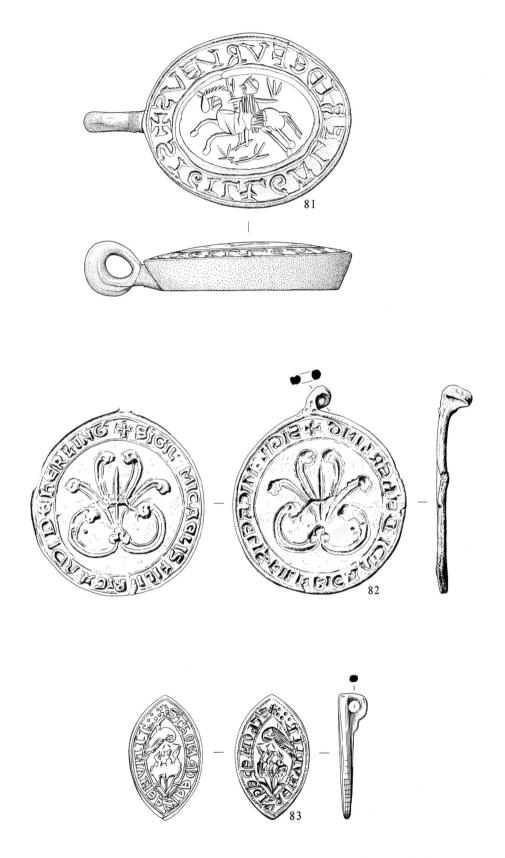

Figure 44 Non-ferrous metal seal matrices nos 81–3. No. 81, scale 2:1; nos 82–3, scale 1:1.

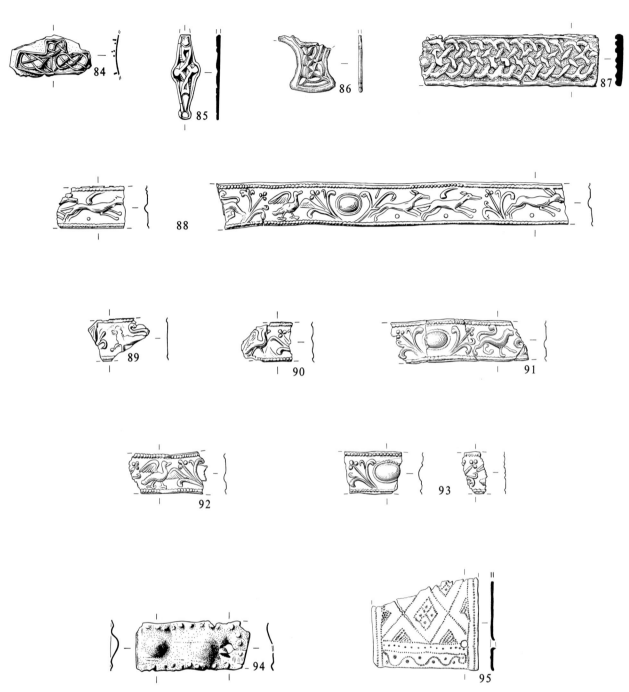

Figure 45 Non-ferrous metal plaques and mounts nos 84–95. Scale 1:1.

Plaques and Mounts

(Fig. 45)

Three fragments of plaques or mounts decorated with interlace were found. The gilded copper alloy fragment with applied wire interlace within a T-shaped cell (84) may once have decorated a casket or a book. Though the wire is plain, the fragment may be compared with the late 10th-century gold plate from Winchester decorated with filigree wire spirals and granules within a filigree sub-rectangular frame (Backhouse *et al.* 1984, cat. no. 78).

The silver-gilt lobed lozenge-shaped fragment (85) has chip-carved interlace, and was possibly the arm of a cross.

The gilded copper alloy cross-shaped mount fragment (86) also has chip-carved interlace ornament, and may be compared with 8th-century mounts with chip-carved ornament from Whitby (Wilson 1964, cat.nos 105–107).

There is a chip-carved cross-shaped brooch from Thetford in the Castle Museum, Norwich (NCM 197.987). Chip-carved ornament on metalwork of this period finds its highest expression on the Witham pins (Wilson 1964, cat. no. 19).

The rectangular cast mount fragment decorated with three-strand interlace and red enamel (87) is probably late 10th or 11th century in date on the basis of the linear non-zoomorphic interlace, seen also on stone sculpture of the period, such as grave-covers. The use of enamel at this period is well attested by the corpus of enamelled disc brooches and mounts (Evison 1977, 1–13; Buckton 1986, 8–18). Red is the least common colour, however.

The fragments of copper alloy repoussé strip (88–93) bear some resemblance in form to repoussé book or box mounts of 8th- or 9th-century date (compare the silver-gilt

Figure 46 Non-ferrous box and casket mounts and fittings nos 96–100. Scale 1:1.

sheet mount from North Elmham, Wade-Martins 1980a, fig. 262, no. 1). In function, they may be compared with the strip decoration on 8th- and 9th-century shrines and reliquaries (*cf.* examples from Dumfriesshire, and the edge strips on the Bischofshofen cross, Webster and Backhouse 1991, cat. nos 133, 135). The decoration with its hunt scene, however, is quite unlike the vine scroll of the Elmham piece, or the inhabited vine scroll of sculpture, manuscript and metalwork, and is much closer to Roman hunt-cup scenes of hounds chasing hares. Roman models were certainly used in Saxon art, as shown by the Romulus and Remus scene on the Larling plaque and the Franks Casket, so the suggestion of a Roman prototype is not implausible.

The mount fragments 94 and 95 are medieval belt-fittings. They are decorated with different ornamental techniques, both in use in the later Middle Ages, repoussé work, and the use of stamped or punched dots.

84. **Gilded sheet fragment** with T-shaped cell made of strip containing applied wire interlace.
SF 87 (T.F.). TL 9787 8501.

85. **Silver-gilt mount** decorated with chip-carved symmetrical single-strand interlace motif.
SF 690 (D.B.). Field north of excavation.

86. **Cross-arm fragment** decorated with chip-carved interlace. Gilded.
SF 214. Topsoil in excavation at 226/510.

87. **Rectangular mount fragment** decorated with three-strand interlace. There are traces of red enamel.
SF 382. Context *216* at 221/530.

88– **Repoussé strip** decorated with oval bosses, sprays of foliage and
93. trefoils, ducks with splayed wings, and hounds chasing hares.
SF 9, 15, 12 (T.F.). Topsoil in 1981 excavation at 209–221/532–537; 277, 228, 291 Context *100,* topsoil in excavation at 209/537, 221/533.

94. **Mount** with two repoussé bosses; borders of small repoussé bosses.
SF 485. Context *447,* upper filling of medieval ditch *667,* at 214/522.

95. **Mount** decorated with tiny stamped dots forming geometric patterns.
SF 256. Topsoil in excavation at 227/519.

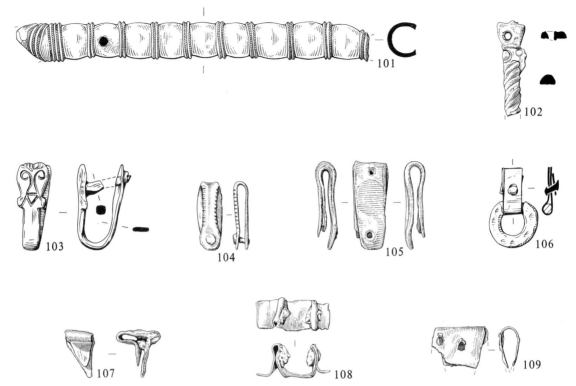

Figure 47 Non-ferrous casket mounts nos 101–2, bindings and clips nos 103–9. Scale 1:1.

Box Mounts
(Figs 46 and 47)
The three sub-triangular mounts belong to a corpus of cast copper alloy mounts, often finely decorated, and often with a flange at the base and iron rivets. An iron strip often survives on the reverse, suggesting the mount may have been riveted in place over an iron binding on a chest or box. It has also been argued convincingly that they are stirrup-mounts (Robinson 1992). Recent finds from Norfolk include several decorated with Late Saxon animal ornament, and many with Anglo-Scandinavian decoration (Margeson 1986, 323– 327).

The Harling examples cover this range of ornament. The crudely engraved face-mask on 96 is unusual. A recent find from Erpingham (County number 12991) has a similar mask. Finely modelled animal masks in relief are known on a number of new finds from Norfolk recorded for the Sites and Monuments Record (a pair from Runhall, SMR no. 25403; one from Brinton, SMR no. 25803; and one from Middleton, SMR no. 24141). All the above mask mounts, and the Harling example, have recently been discussed and illustrated (Ashley *et al.* 1991)

The three-armed mount (97) with animal-head terminals and its traces of niello and silver wire inlay, was obviously a very fine example.

There are substantial traces of iron on the reverse of both 96 and 97. The other mount (98) is unlike the main corpus as it appears to have had no flange and is only very slightly convex. There is a broken rivet hole at one end; the other end is damaged. Like 97, there are traces of silver wire inlaid in the animal bodies. The ornament is Ringerike-style, with the characteristic pendant lobe between two elongated animal heads. Tendrils branch from the animal heads and the ribbon-like bodies interlace with each other and with at least one other animal whose smaller head lies at one edge of the mount. The same motif of a pair of animal heads with a pendant lobe between can

be seen on a recent find of a horse-harness decorative pendant fragment (?Norwich, now in the Castle Museum, Norwich 401.985). The reverse of the mount has uneven ridges from casting.

The openwork hasp (99) is probably 10th/11th century on grounds of similarity with openwork strap-ends of that date (*cf.* 75).

The hooked fitting (100) may have been used to secure a casket or a belt or may possibly have been used on horse-harness. It is 12th/13th century.

The gilded, cast copper alloy half-round binding (101) with pairs of moulded ribs is likely to be from the overhanging lid of a casket or possibly the edge of a book-cover. One end is wedge-shaped and here the ribs are in two groups of three, one curved close to the other. This end was shaped to fit the next part of the binding, possibly at a corner. It may be early medieval, 11th or 12th century. But similar bindings are found on Middle and Late Saxon reliquaries and book-covers, so the possibility of an earlier date must not be ruled out.

The ribbed strip (102) is a medieval casket mount.

96. **Sub-triangular mount** with flange at base, and hole for attachment at terminal. Engraved face-mask. Two rivet holes with iron traces at base. Iron under flange.
SF 91 (T.F.). Tl 9803 8519.

97. **Sub-triangular mount** with three projecting arms in the form of animal heads. Central rivet hole with iron stain under it; iron on reverse under flange; two iron rivets through flange. Body of mount with double-contoured border inlaid with niello and silver wire.
SF 712 (T.F.). TL 9795 8487.

98. **Sub-triangular mount** with rivet hole at one end, broken at the other end. Decorated with cast ornament in the form of two animals with pendant lobe between the heads, and interlacing bodies. Traces of silver wire inlaid in animal bodies.
SF 272. Topsoil in excavation at 233/530.

99. **Openwork plate** with outer frame decorated with projecting knobs.
SF 625 (T.F.). Field north of excavation, at TL 9805 8518.

100. **Gilded hooked fitting** with lobed moulded terminal pierced with a rivet-hole; rivet through moulded panel above hook.
SF 637 (T.F.). South of Church Clump.

101. Gilded binding fragment with moulded decoration in the form of zones of double ribs; one rivet hole.
SF 241. Topsoil in excavation at 209/514.
102. Lead or pewter strip with rivet hole in expanded end; cast twisted decoration.
SF 210. Topsoil in excavation at 225/507.

Bindings and Clips
(Fig. 47)
103–109 are decorated bindings and sheet clips from caskets or vessels. The fitting with the engraved stylised face (103) may be 11th century and was probably used to suspend keys or toilet articles. The others are medieval.

103. Looped fitting with integral shank, engraved with stylised face.
SF 640 (T.F.). South of Church Clump.
104. Folded sheet clip with nicked edges; rivet securing open end.
SF 294. Topsoil in excavation at 205/520.
105. Folded sheet clip; two rivet holes.
SF 212. Topsoil in excavation at 214/513.
106. Folded sheet clip with iron ring.
SF 591. Spoil heap from excavation.
107. Folded sheet clip.
SF 247. Topsoil in excavation at 209/518.
108. Folded sheet clip.
SF 296. Topsoil in excavation at 232/544.

109. Folded sheet clip.
SF 313. Context 105, at 232/511.

Studs
(Fig. 48)
Studs from belts or caskets include a 13th-century gilded one in the form of a crowned bearded head (111).

110. Gilded stud with integral shank; crowned bearded head, with engraved features.
SF 11 (T.F.). Topsoil in 1981 trench.
111. Stud with circular head, pelleted repoussé border.
SF 571. Context 775, at 229/537.
112. Stud with slightly convex rectangular head.
SF 535. Context 650, filling of medieval ditch 669 at 218/520.
113. Stud with gilded, slightly convex rectangular head.
SF 316. Context 714, filling of medieval ditch 138 at 230/518.
114. Stud with hemispherical head decorated with incised cross.
SF 312. Context 105, at 232/510.
115. Stud with hemispherical head.
SF 254. Topsoil in excavation at 213/517.
116. Stud with hemispherical head.
SF 264. Topsoil in excavation at 206/532.
117. Stud with rectangular head.
SF 223. Topsoil in excavation at 209/531.
118 Pair of heavy-duty studs with hemispherical heads and engraved
and with star motifs.
119. SF 289 and 253. Topsoil in excavation at 231/513 and 233/519.

Balance
(Fig. 49)
An arm from a folding balance (120) has a wire loop for suspension at one end; a hinged beam with a central pointer would have been attached to the rivet hole at the other end, and by a rivet in the other arm, allowing the arms to be folded up if necessary.

120. Balance arm fragment with wire suspension loop through hole in collared circular terminal; arm broken at rivet hole at other end.
SF 96 (T.F.). TL 9805 8522.

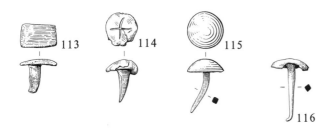

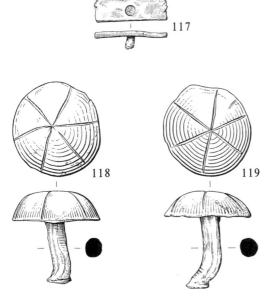

Figure 48 Non-ferrous studs nos 110–19. Scale 1:1.

Figure 49 Non-ferrous balance arm no. 120. Scale 1:1.

Lead Spindle-whorls
(Fig. 50)
121–126 are conical spindle-whorls, 121 is decorated with incised cross-hatching. 127 is discoidal. Both conical and discoidal lead spindle-whorls are known from medieval contexts, including Bryggen, Norway (Øye 1988, 50). They occurred there in contexts from before 1170 to 1413. Two are decorated, one with a diagonal lattice pattern (Øye 1988, fig. II, 14).

Conical
121. Decorated with incised cross-hatching.
SF 14 (T.F.). Topsoil in 1981 trench.
122. SF 476. Context 447, at 220/524.
123. SF 474. Context 447, upper filling of Late Saxon phase of ditch 700 at 203/529.
124. SF 290. Context 100, topsoil in excavation at 229/539.
125. SF 323. Context 105, at 227/522.
126. SF 537. Context 664, filling of medieval ditch 700, at 216/523.

Discoidal
127. SF 583. Context 785, filling of medieval ditch 852 at 232/530.

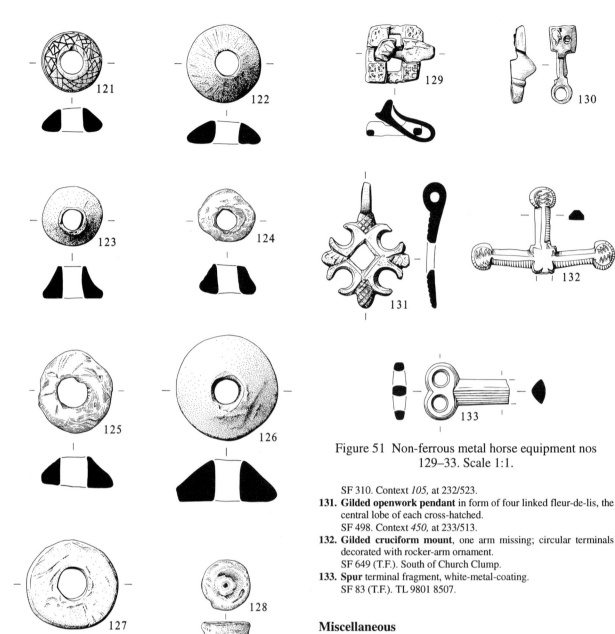

Figure 50 Lead spindle-whorls nos 121–7 and weight no.
128. Scale 1:1.

Lead Weight
(Fig. 50)
The tapering cylindrical object (128) may be a weight.

128. Tapering cylindrical object.
   SF 267. Topsoil in excavation at 219/528.

Horse Equipment
(Fig. 51)
The horse equipment is medieval, and consists of two harness pendants (129, 131), a suspension loop for a pendant (130), a cruciform mount (132), and a spur terminal (133). The openwork pendant is similar to one from Castle Acre Castle (Goodall, A.R. 1982, fig. 44, no. 35).

129. Gilded square pendant with decorated corner fields.
   SF 663 (D.B.). Field north of excavation.
130. Stud with suspension loop for pendant.

Figure 51 Non-ferrous metal horse equipment nos
129–33. Scale 1:1.

SF 310. Context *105,* at 232/523.
131. Gilded openwork pendant in form of four linked fleur-de-lis, the central lobe of each cross-hatched.
   SF 498. Context *450,* at 233/513.
132. Gilded cruciform mount, one arm missing; circular terminals decorated with rocker-arm ornament.
   SF 649 (T.F.). South of Church Clump.
133. Spur terminal fragment, white-metal-coating.
   SF 83 (T.F.). TL 9801 8507.

Miscellaneous
(Fig. 52)
134. Awl. Late Bronze Age.
   SF 358. Filling of post-medieval pit *174,* at 207/543.
135. Offcut, with border of stamped pellets. Medieval.
   SF 239. Topsoil in excavation at 200/515.
136. Spherical weight with iron core and copper alloy coating. Two concentric circles of stamped annulets on one face. Stamped dots forming triangles on body of object. Weight 20.02gms.
   This is of Late Saxon date. Several similar examples have recently been recorded from other Norfolk sites with Saxon assemblages, as at Great Walsingham (SMR site 28254) and Hindringham (SMR site 24909). These carry weight marks indicated by different numbers of circles within the two concentric circles of stamped annulets.
   A group of five weights, with weight marks and graded in size, was excavated in a 10th-century grave in Hemlingby, Gästrikland, Sweden (Roesdahl (ed.) 1992, 266, cat. no. 151). Because of the iron corrosion on the marked face of the Harling example, it is impossible to decipher whether there are weight marks within the two concentric circles.
   SF 279. Topsoil in excavation at 207/525.
137. Circular mount, engraved quatrefoil, two tiny rivet holes. Medieval belt or box mount.
   SF 305. Context *105,* at 228/516.
138. Sheet hook fragment.
   SF 478. Context *447,* at 220/524.
139. Strip with spiral terminal.
   SF 314. Context *105,* at 230/520.

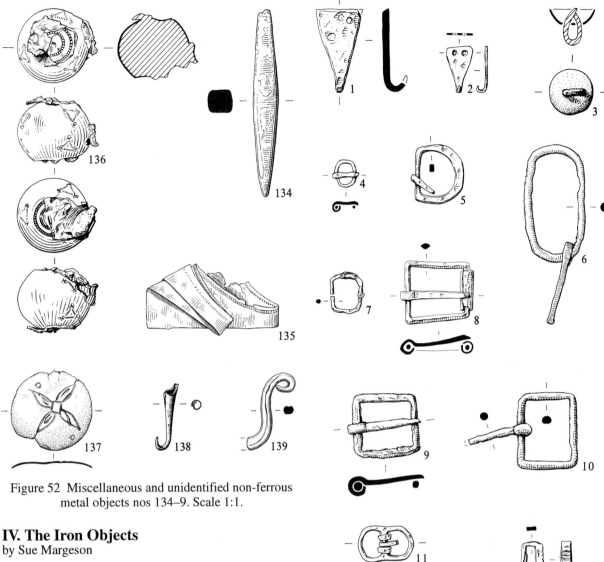

Figure 52 Miscellaneous and unidentified non-ferrous
metal objects nos 134–9. Scale 1:1.

IV. The Iron Objects
by Sue Margeson

Dress Fittings
(Fig. 53)

Triangular hooked tags made of iron (1, 2) are less
common than the copper alloy ones. Like the undecorated
copper alloy examples (41–44), they are likely to be 10th
or 11th century in date.

D-shaped buckles are the most common type of iron
buckle, known in both Late Saxon and medieval contexts
(Goodall 1993, cat. nos 181–195).

Rectangular buckles were popular in post-medieval
contexts, and often had sheet rollers to ease the sliding of
the belt (8).

1. **Hooked tag.**
   SF 53. Brown soil in 1981 trench.
2. **Hooked tag.**
   SF 350. Context *150,* at 227/512.
3. **Button base** with iron loop.
   SF 589. Context *793,* at 233/541.
4. **Oval buckle** with tongue.
   SF 354. Context *153,* at 212/531.
5. **D-shaped buckle** with tongue.
   SF 321. Context *130,* filling of pit 589 at 229/524.
6. **Oval buckle** (large) with tongue.
   SF 330. Context *153,* at 211/529.
7. **'Oval' buckle frame.**
   SF 335. Context *153,* at 205/533.
8. **Rectangular buckle** with sheet roller over bar.
   SF 484. Context *447,* at 216/523.
9. **Rectangular buckle.**

Figure 53 Iron dress fittings nos 1–12. Scale 1:2.

SF 266. Topsoil in excavation at 233/526.
10. **Rectangular buckle.**
    SF 344. Context *153,* at 212/541.
11. **Double-looped buckle** remains of pin.
    SF 268. Topsoil in excavation at 228/529.
12. **Belt-slide,** with ends folded over, and ridged decoration.
    SF 384. Context *218,* at 204/531.

Rings, Chains and Escutcheons
(Fig. 54)

Rings (13–17) were used for a wide variety of household
purposes, such as furniture handles, or as parts of chains
(18), used to suspend cauldrons or other hearth equipment.
They might also have been used for horse-harness or as
belt-fittings. The escutcheon was probably used for a
vessel handle (19).

13. **Ring.**
    SF 499. Context *450,* at 232/514.
14. Penannular **ring.**
    SF 526. Context *554,* at 220/523.
15. **Ring.**
    SF 536. Context *654,* filling of junction of ditches *139* and *611,* at
    224/517.

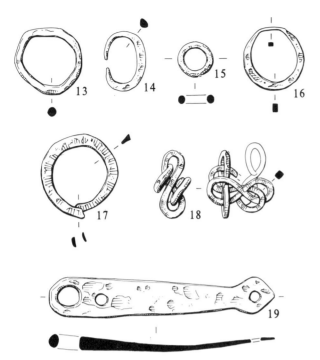

Figure 54 Iron rings, chains and escutcheons nos 13–9.
Scale 1:2.

16. Ring (one facet — possibly a buckle).
SF 42. Above pit *367* at 216/532.
17. Ring, flattened section, overlapping ends.
SF 299. Context *103,* at 224/529.
18. Chain links.
SF 477. Context *447,* at 220/524.
19. Escutcheon.
SF 377. Context *216,* at 215/528.

Strike-a-lights
(Fig. 55)
Two-armed strike-a-lights with spiral terminals are known
from 10th-century contexts (Graham-Campbell 1980, cat.
no. 24).

20. Strike-a-light with spiral terminals and cusped inner edge.
SF 452. Context *446,* at 229/529.
21. Strike-a-light terminal fragment.
SF 698 (D.B.). Field north of excavation.

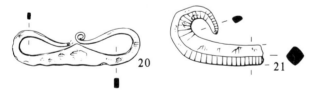

Figure 55 Iron strike-a-lights nos 20–1. Scale 1:2.

Implements
(Fig. 56)
Three-pronged flesh-forks are known from medieval
contexts, both with hooked prongs set at the end of the
shaft as here, and straight prongs set along the shaft as on
one from Pottergate (Atkin *et al* 1985, fig. 40, no. 38).
They are shown in use in manuscripts (such as the Luttrell
Psalter, British Library Add. Ms. 42130, f.207).
Fish-hooks are a common find in medieval contexts.

22. Flesh fork.
SF 391. Context *238,* at 210/530.
23. Fish-hook.
SF 436. Context *446,* at 228/540.

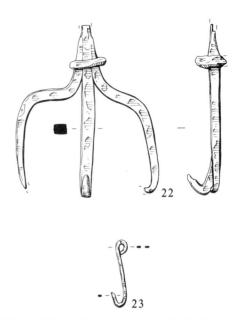

Figure 56 Iron implements nos 22–3. Scale 1:2.

Pivoting Knives
(Fig. 57)
The double-ended blade, set between a pair of riveted
plates or scales, swivelled on a rivet which holds plates
and blade together. An adjacent rivet acted as a stop for
whichever end of the blade was not in use. Pivoting knives
have been excavated at Thetford (Goodall, I.H. 1984, fig.
122, nos 782, 783), Norwich (Goodall, I.H. 1993, cat. nos
782, 783), and a complete one from Canterbury
(Graham-Campbell 1980, cat. no. 473, where a diagram
illustrates their use). They are usually dated to the 9th or
10th century. Two other examples were recovered from
grave 451.

24. Pivoting knife.
SF 446. Context *446,* at 232/534.

Whittle-tang Knives
(Fig. 57)
Whittle-tang knives with angled backs and tips (25–32)
are well known in Late Saxon contexts (Goodall 1984, fig.
122, nos 50–53, fig. 123, nos 54– 62). The other knives
(33–42) include several variants of the type.

25– Knives with angled backs and tips.
32.
25. SF 613. South of Church Clump.
26. SF 558. Context *754,* filling of medieval ditch *611* at 222/512.
27. SF 487. Context *447,* at 212/517.
28. SF 262. Topsoil in excavation at 204/532.
29. SF 445. Context *446,* at 226/536.
30. SF 336. Context *153,* at 202/536.
31. SF 275. Topsoil in excavation at 206/533.
32. SF 426. Context *408,* upper filling of medieval ditch at 220/526.
33. Knife with angled back, curved tip, cutting edge curved at shoulder
through sharpening.
SF 415. Context *341,* at 218/526.
34. Knife with angled back, broken tip.
SF 369. Context *210,* at 217/538.
35. Knife with angled back, broken tip, cutting edge curved at shoulder
through sharpening.
SF 393. Backfilling of 1981 trench.
36. Knife with angled back, broken tip.
SF 522. Context *541,* at 219/511.
37. Knife with long tang set at base of shoulder, angled back.
SF 385. Context *230,* upper filling of ditch 700, at 202/528.
38. Knife with angled back.
SF 405. Context *298,* at 222/530.

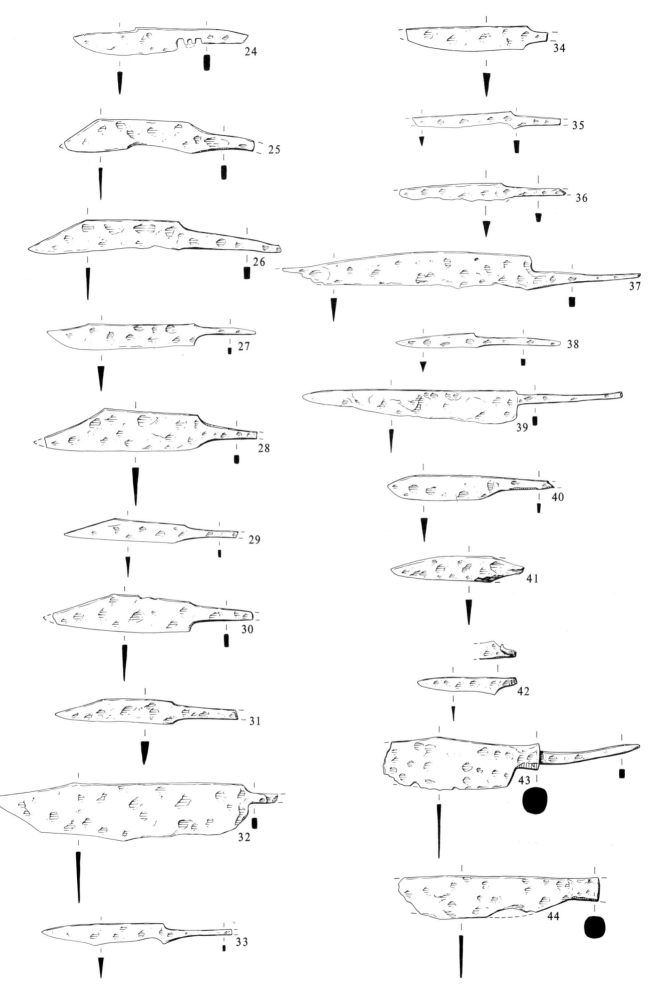

Figure 57 Iron knives nos 24–44. Scale 1:2.

39. Knife with whittle tang set just below back, straight shoulder.
SF 479. Context *447,* upper filling of junction of ditches *611* and *700* at 220/524.
40. Knife with straight back, slightly angled tip.
SF 610. South of Church Clump.
41. Knife fragment with angled back and tip.
SF 211. Topsoil in excavation 223/509.
42. Knife blade with straight back; tang folded over through damage.
SF 208. Topsoil in excavation at 208/513.

Whittle-tang Knives with Bolsters
(Fig. 57)

Bolsters, introduced in the mid-16th century, are a common feature of 17th-century knives. The bolster removed the need for shoulder plates (Goodall 1993, cat. nos 867–882).

43. Knife with bolster and whittle tang.
SF 609. South of Church Clump.
44. Knife with bolster, tang broken.
SF 608. Context *25,* south of Church Clump.

Shears
(Fig. 58)

Shears with looped bows are known in pre- and post-Conquest contexts (Thetford, Goodall 1984, fig. 126, nos 107–110).

45. Shears with looped bow.
SF 43. Filling of pit *367,* 1981 trench.
46. Shears with looped bow.
SF 465. Context *447,* upper filling of junction of ditches *604* and *611,* at 224/524.

Vessel Handle
(Fig. 59)

47. Handle fragment with attachment plate.
SF 203. Topsoil in excavation at 230/502.

Structural Ironwork

Staples
(Fig. 60)

Staples were used to secure bolts on door jambs, to bind timbers together, to hold chains and hasps in place around buildings, or to fasten the ends of handles on chests and other furniture (*cf.* 82).

48. U-shaped staple.
SF 422. Context *377,* filling of junction of ditches *700* and *852,* at 234/526.
49. ?Staple.
SF 459. Context *446,* at 230/526.
50. Rectangular staple.
SF 413. Context *337,* at 222/525.
51. U-shaped staple.
SF 458. Context *446,* at 230/527.
52. U-shaped staple.
SF 450. Context *446,* at 227/530.
53. U-shaped staple.
SF 494. Context *448,* upper filling of ditch *700.*
54. U-shaped staple.
SF 488. Context *447,* spit in brown soil at 211/511.
55. Plate with strip with incurved end.
SF 423. Context *390,* filling of ditch *352* at 224/528.
56. Rectangular staple with incurved end.
SF 501. Context *450,* at 228/517.
57. Rectangular staple with incurved end.
SF 442. Context *446,* at 231/535.

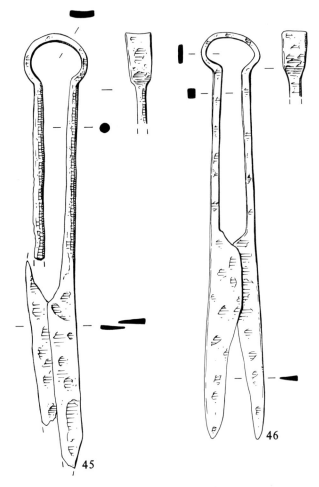

Figure 58 Iron shears nos 45–6. Scale 1:2.

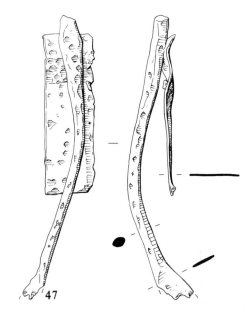

Figure 59 Iron vessel handle no. 47. Scale 1:2.

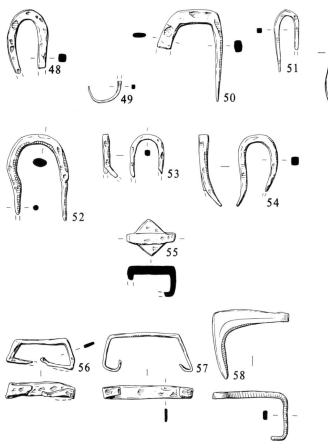

Figure 60 Iron staples nos 48–57 and wall-hook no. 58.
Scale 1:2.

Wall-hooks
(Fig. 60)
The tips were clenched round and embedded in timber to secure the hook (Goodall 1984, fig. 128, nos 134–5).
58. Wall-hook.
   SF 343. Context *153,* at 215/539.

Hinge Pivots
(Fig. 61)
These were used with wood, or were driven into joints between masonry.
59. Hinge pivot.
   SF 602. Context *554,* at 220/524.
60. Hinge pivot.
   SF 475. Context *447,* at 220/508.
61. Hinge terminal with rivet hole.
   SF 612. South of Church Clump.
62. Hinge with hanging eye and two rivets.
   SF 482. Context *447,* at 216/510.

Binding Strips from Caskets or Furniture
(Fig. 61)
63. Strip with rivet.
   SF 574. Context *778,* at 232/533.
64. Strip with two rivets.
   SF 45a. Filling of pit *367,* 1981 trench.
65. Strip with hole and curved end.
   SF 50. Brown soil in 1981 trench.
66. Strip with rivet in circular terminal, wood adhering.
   SF 562. Context *768,* at 205/520.
67. Folded strip with two rivet holes.
   SF 432. Context *446,* at 230/543.
68. Folded strip.
   SF 45b. Filling of pit *367,* 1981 trench.
69. Strip with curved ends, rivet hole at each end.
   SF 573. Context *778,* at 231/533.
70. Quatrefoil mount with central rivet.
   SF 317. Context *116,* filling of medieval ditch *604* at 232/523.

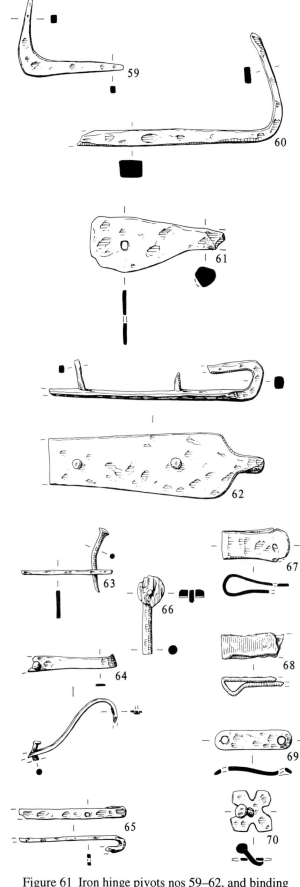

Figure 61 Iron hinge pivots nos 59–62, and binding strips nos 63–70. Scale 1:2.

Keys
(Fig. 62)

The double-pronged latch-lifter was the simplest sort of key, known from both Roman and early and Late Saxon contexts. The barrel padlock keys may be compared with some from Thetford (Goodall 1984, fig. 132, nos 180–182). The other keys (74–76) are medieval types.

71. '**Latch-lifter**'.
SF 355. Context *153*, spit in brown soil at 201/532.
72. **Barrel padlock key** with suspension ring.
SF 566. Context *775*, at 226/538.
73. **Barrel padlock key** with suspension ring, bit missing, expanded terminal.
SF 565. Context *676*, at 228/530.
74. **Key** with lozenge-shaped bow, solid stem, bit rolled in one with stem.
SF 527. Context *588*, filling of pit *589* at 230/524.
75. **Key** with circular bow, hollow stem, bit rolled in one with stem.
SF 44, filling of pit *367*, 1981 trench.
76. **Key** with circular collared bow, solid stem, bit rolled in one with stem.
SF 200 (T.F.). Context *100*.

Barrel Padlock
(Fig. 63)

The barrel padlock is widely known from medieval contexts such as Pottergate, Norwich (Atkin *et al* 1985, fig. 144, no. 69), but they are also known from Late Saxon contexts as at York (Hall 1984, fig. 129).

77. **Barrel padlock** with cylindrical case, padlock bolt missing.
SF 325. Context *153*, at 214/525.

Box Fittings
(Fig. 64)

These objects have been grouped together as they may come from the same box. Nos 78 and 80–84 were found in Context *448*, the upper filling of medieval ditch *700* at 205/519 and No.79 came from Context *214*, a spit of brown soil above the ditch, at the same co-ordinates.

78. **Handle fragment,** terminal hooked through hole in attachment strip which has circular terminal, and twisted shaft.
SF 471.
79. **Attachment strip** fragment with circular terminal, twisted shaft.
SF 373.
80. **Attachment strip** fragment with twisted shaft.
SF 468.
81. **Handle fragment,** terminal hooked through hole in attachment plate.
SF 469.
82. **Rectangular hasp** secured by two U-shaped staples.
SF 467.
83. **Lock-plate.**
SF 467.
84. **Binding strip** with wood inside.
SF 470.

Miscellaneous Structural Ironwork
(Fig. 65)

Looped spikes were driven into joints in masonry to hold door jambs in place, or into timber posts possibly to hold candlesticks, to secure hangings, or for other purposes.

85. **Bar,** twisted, ?part of handle.
SF 333. Context *153*, at 210/534.
86. **Spike** with looped terminal.
SF 448. Context *446*, at 229/533.
87. **Spike** with looped terminal.
SF 503a. Context *450*, at 228/517.
88. **Spike** with pierced terminal.
SF 503b. Context as No.87.
89. **Spike** with looped terminal, from which ring with attachment plate is suspended.
SF 368. Context *203*, filling of post-medieval bone pit *169*.

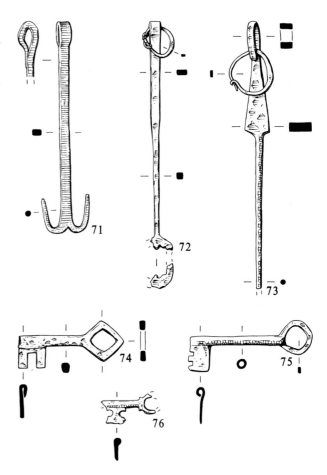

Figure 62 Iron keys nos 71–6. Scale 1:2.

Heckle
(Fig. 66)

Heckles were used to prepare wool and flax fibres for spinning. This type of comb is probably medieval, and may be compared with examples from Pottergate, Norwich (Atkin *et al* 1985, fig. 46, nos 80–82).

90. **Heckle comb binding** with teeth; wooden block inside sheet binding.
SF 349. Context *153*, spit in brown soil at 213/544.

Comb Teeth
(Figs 66 and 67)

These can be circular (91–95, 97, 98) or rectangular in section (96).

91– SF 338, 345 and 346. Context *153*, at 209/535, 211/541 and 210/
3. 542.
94. SF 486. Context *447*, at 213/516.
95– SF 496 and 497. Context *449*, at 216/543 and 210/542.
6.
97. SF 402. Context *289*, at 221/530.
98. SF 412. Context *337*, at 222/529.

Metal-working Tool
(Fig. 68)

Blacksmiths used sets to cut cold or hot iron. Because of its small size this piece was probably used for hot iron. Sets changed little in the Saxon and medieval periods and so are difficult to date.

99. **Set.**
SF 348. Context *153*, at 207/540.

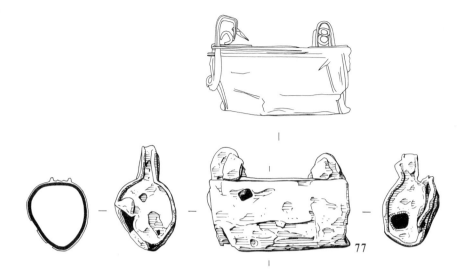

Figure 63 Iron barrel padlock no. 77. Scale 1:2.

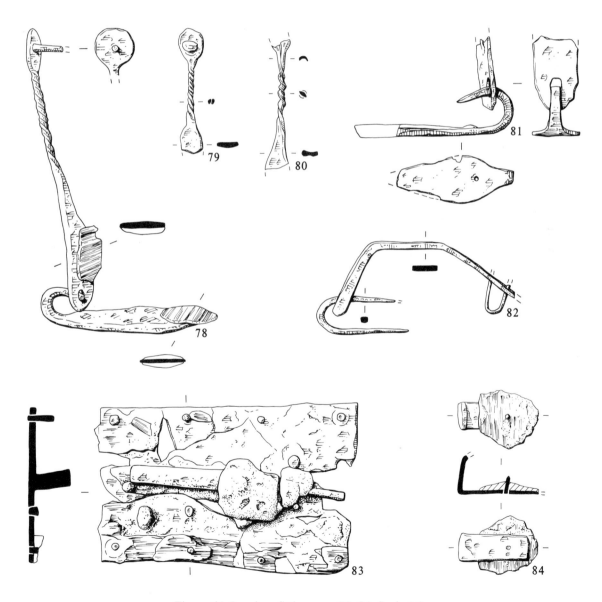

Figure 64 Iron box fittings nos 78–84. Scale 1:2.

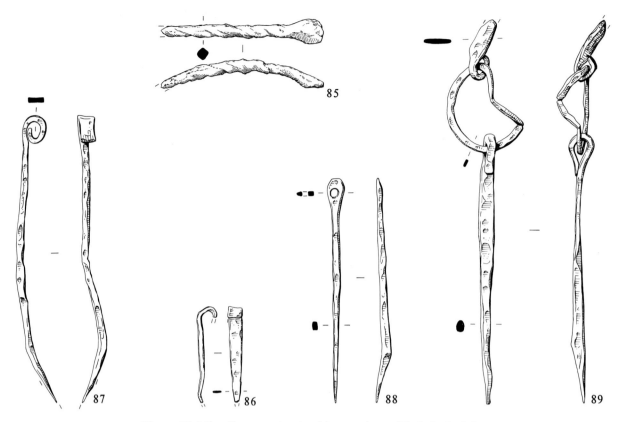

Figure 65 Miscellaneous structural ironwork nos 85–9. Scale 1:2.

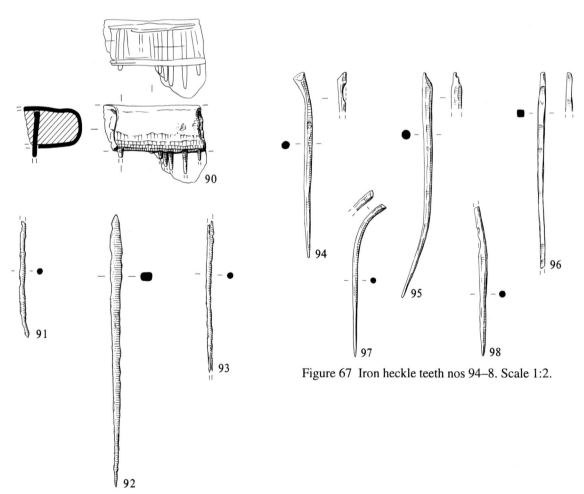

Figure 67 Iron heckle teeth nos 94–8. Scale 1:2.

Figure 66 Iron heckle no. 90 and heckle teeth nos 91–3.
Scale 1:2.

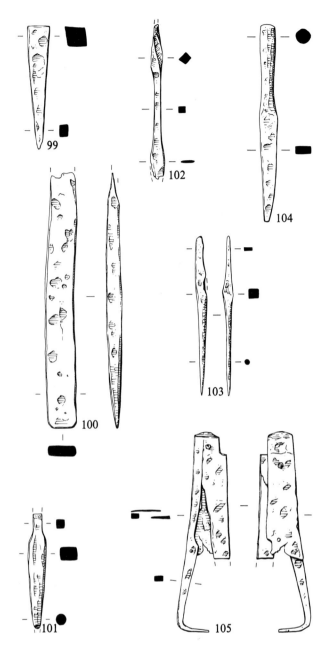

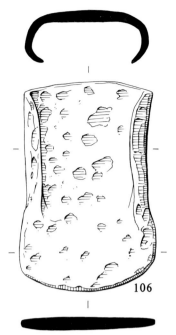

Figure 69 Plough iron no. 106. Scale 1:2.

Figure 68 Blacksmith's iron set no. 99, and iron wood-working tools nos 100–5. Scale 1:2.

Wood-working Tools
(Fig. 68)

Reamers were used to clean out or enlarge holes bored in wood by augers. Callipers were used to measure work. The awl and the punch were probably also used for wood-working. Like the metal-working tools, these changed little, and are difficult to date.

100. Chisel.
SF 489. Context *447,* at 211/512.

101. Reamer.
SF 504. Context *450,* at 233/523.

102. Auger with twisted shaft, broken spoon bit.
SF 586. Context *785,* filling of medieval ditch *852* at 233/530.

103. Awl.
SF 551. Context *750,* at 209/516.

104. Punch.
SF 540. Context *707,* filling of probably medieval grave-like feature at 209/513.

105. Callipers.
SF 611. Context *25,* south of Church Clump.

Agricultural Tool
(Fig. 69)

The plough iron with its wedge-shaped blade is probably medieval. Late Saxon plough irons have triangular blades, compare an example from Thetford (Goodall 1984, fig. 121, no. 43).

106. Plough iron.
SF 390. Context *218,* at 206/530.

Horse Equipment
(Fig. 70)

Bridle side-links of similar type come from Late Saxon contexts at Thetford (Goodall 1984, fig. 138, 258–261). There is a complete example of an iron snaffle-bit from York with similar side-links (Waterman 1959, fig. 8, no. 1).

107. Bridle side-link.
SF 449. Context *446,* at 233/534.

108. Bridle side-link.
SF 533. Context *544,* at 220/518.

109. Bridle side-link, decorated with projecting lobes.
SF 483. Context *447,* at 216/517.

Weapons
(Fig. 71

The arrowheads could have been used for both military and hunting purposes. Javelins with squat blades are known from 11th-century contexts (Goodall 1993, cat. no. 1859).

110. Leaf-shaped arrowhead with socket.
SF 31. 1981 trench.

111. Leaf-shaped arrowhead with socket.
SF 481. Context *447,* at 219/520.

112. Leaf-shaped arrowhead with socket.
SF 447. Context *446,* at 229/534.

113. Barbed arrowhead with socket.
SF 328. Context *153,* at 213/528.

114. Barbed arrowhead with socket.
SF 461. Context *446,* at 233/525.

115. Barbed arrowhead, socket broken.
SF 80 (T.F.). Field north of excavation.

116. Javelin blade fragment with non-ferrous metal plating on each side of midrib.
SF 206. Topsoil in excavation at 216/504.

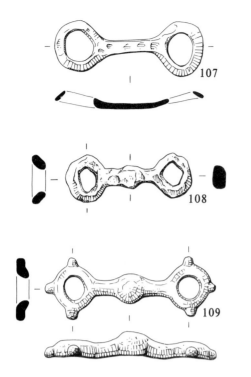

Figure 70 Iron bridle side-links nos 107–9. Scale 1:2.

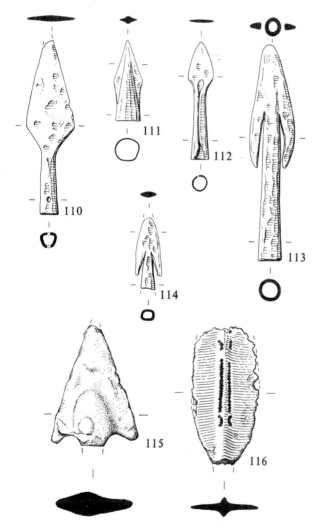

Figure 71 Iron weapons nos 110–6. Scale 1:2, except no. 115, scale 1:1.

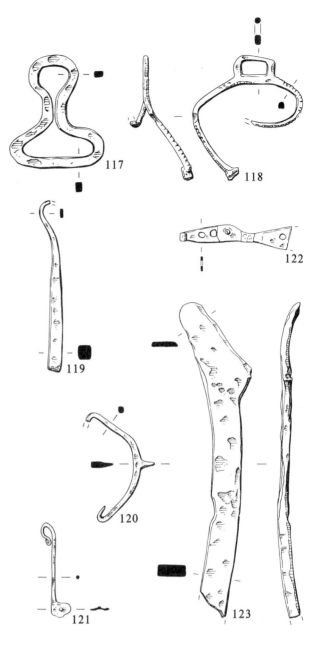

Figure 72 Miscellaneous iron objects nos 117–23.
Scale 1:2.

Miscellaneous
(Fig. 72)

117. Figure-of-eight-shaped link, ?harness or other attachment chain.
SF 35. Brown soil in 1981 trench.

118. Looped decorated ?harness or other fitting.
SF 480. Context *447*, at 219/510.

119. Strip.
SF 428. Context *419*, filling of post-hole in east wall of Late Saxon building B, at 221/531.

120. Spiked rod with incurved arms.
SF 518. Context *517*, filling of pit *600*, at 231/524.

121. Strip with looped terminal and attachment.
SF 513. Context *517*, as No.121, at 232/524.

122. Strip with rivet holes.
SF 425. Context *405*, filling of medieval ditch *700* at 223/528.

123. Strip with one curved terminal.
SF 490. Context *448*, filling of medieval ditch *700* at 206/524.

V. Fired Clay Object
(Fig. 73)
by Sue Margeson

Loomweight fragment.
SF 505. Context *452,* at 232/520.

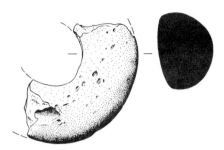

Figure 73 Fired clay loomweight fragment. Scale 1:2.

VI. Stone Object
(Fig. 74)
by Sue Margeson

Whetstone with two partially drilled holes.
SF 226. Context *100,* topsoil in excavation at 227/529.

Figure 74 Whetstone fragment. Scale 1:2.

VII. Bone Objects
(Fig. 75)
by Sue Margeson

Pig fibula needles may have been used for coarse netting, or as rough dress pins with a thong or cord through the hole tied to the point once it has passed through the fabric (MacGregor 1985, 120–1).

Double-ended bone implements may have been used as pin-beaters to straighten the weft threads during weaving, but other functions have been suggested such as burnishers or styli (Rogerson and Dallas 1984, 170, figs 191–3).

1. Pig fibula **needle or pin**.
   SF 416. Context *341,* at 216/531.
2–4. Three roughly shaped **double-ended implements**, polished through use (one broken).
   SFs 547, 550, 407. Contexts *676* and *298,* at 227/530, 227/531 and 222/530.

VIII. Objects from Burial *451*
(Fig. 76)
by Sue Margeson

The locations of the artefacts in the grave are plotted on Fig. 22.

The copper alloy buckle with a rectangular moulded frame (1) may be compared with moulded buckles from

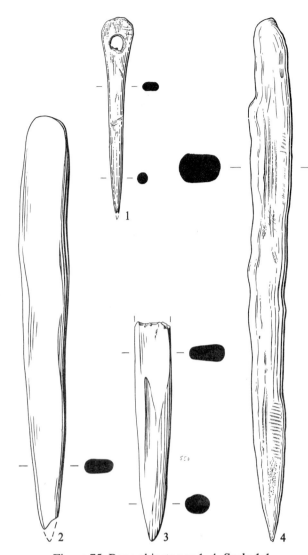

Figure 75 Bone objects nos 1–4. Scale 1:1.

Viking graves elsewhere, though the rectangular frame is unusual. D-shaped iron buckles (2) are more common.

The decoration on the ear-scoop (3) is very fine, with leaf-shaped zones divided by transverse ribbing. Ear-scoops are unusual finds at this period (compare an elaborate silver one from Birka in Sweden, and one in a set of copper alloy toilet implements from Hedeby, Germany (Graham-Campbell 1980, cat. nos 176, 177), whereas other toilet articles, such as tweezers and combs, are not.

Pivoting knives (4, 5) are usually dated to the 9th or 10th century, which helps confirm the date of this grave. Another pivoting knife was found elsewhere on the site (24).

The whittle-tang knife with the long tang (6) is also a pre-Conquest Scandinavian type, and may be compared with several from Thetford (Goodall, I.H. 1984, fig. 124, nos 84–89, fig. 125, nos 90–92).

Whittle-tang knives with angled backs (7) are known from Late Saxon contexts, and there is a group from elsewhere on the site (25–38). Whetstones (8) are commonly found in accompanied male burials.

The prick spur with its straight sides (9) may be compared with Late Saxon spurs from Thetford (Ellis

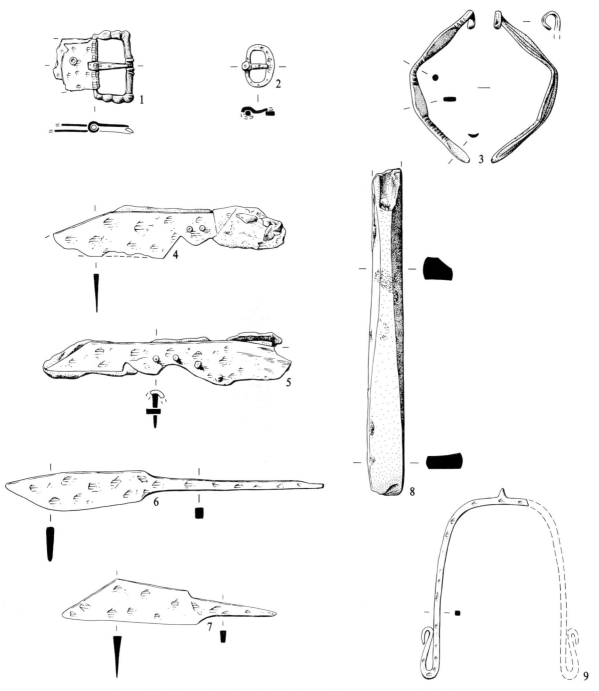

Figure 76 Objects from burial *451*. Scale 1:2; except no. 3, Scale 1:1.

1984, fig. 140, nos 266–270), though the terminals are unusual.

This accompanied burial of the late 9th or early 10th century is of great importance. Because of its date, it must be the burial of a pagan Viking settler, presumably one of the first generation of settlers. The Vikings were soon converted to Christianity. It is only the third Viking burial known in East Anglia, the others being at Saffron Walden, Essex, and Santon Downham, Norfolk.

1. **Copper alloy rectangular buckle** with moulded frame; sheet buckle-plate; pin looped over frame.
   SF 495.
2. **Iron D-shaped buckle**; pin looped over frame.
   SF 555.
3. **Copper alloy ear-scoop** with broken loop at other end. Decorated with zones of transverse ribbing.
   SF 554.
4. **Iron pivoting knife**.
   SF 492.
5. **Iron pivoting knife**.
   SF 492.
6. **Iron straight-backed knife** with angled tip and long whittle tang.
   SF 492.
7. **Iron knife** with angled back, whittle tang.
   SF 491
8. **Whetstone**.
   SF 493.
9. **Iron spur** with straight sides and unusual curled-round terminals.
   SF 556.

IX. Iron Slag
by Justine Bayley

A small group of assorted material was examined and the individual samples identified. The total weight was 3.6kg and all fragments were from medieval or unstratified contexts. As well as fuel ash slag and smithing slag, which are regularly found on most occupation sites, Middle Harling produced a single fragment of tap slag and a number of pieces of fayalitic slag which are denser than smithing slags but do not have the flowed structure of tap slag. These were all fragments of fairly large blocks and were probably produced in non-tapping smelting furnaces.

The variable nature and small quantity of the slag samples suggest that iron was not actually being worked in the area excavated but that both smithing and smelting had been carried out nearby. Two different smelting technologies are suggested, the dense iron slag coming from a non-tapping furnace, probably of Saxon date, while the tap slag would have come from a tapped furnace of either Roman or medieval date.

X. Lava Quern
(not illustrated)

Rhineland lava quern fragments weighing 9.47kg were found in seventy-two contexts, of which twenty-nine were sealed. The earliest stratified contexts containing lava were Late Saxon in date. Most of the pieces were comminuted fragments, while the largest piece, weighing 448gm, was recovered from the ploughsoil before the excavation. No diameters were measurable.

XI. The Pottery
(Figs 77 and 78)

For prehistoric pottery, see Chapter 2, I. Prehistoric Occupation, p.40–5.

Roman
Sixty-three sherds are predominantly greyware of the late 1st and 2nd centuries. Later Roman wares are scarce but include three sherds of Nene Valley colour-coated and an Oxfordshire red-slipped bowl rim sherd.

Middle Saxon
With the exception of five imported sherds described below, all the Middle Saxon pottery appeared to be products of the Ipswich kilns, with the range of forms and fabrics closely following the Ipswich pattern (West 1963). A bowl rim, of varying profile, in Ipswich sandy fabric is illustrated (Fig. 77, No. 1) as is an Ipswich body sherd, also in sandy fabric, which is decorated with an apparently double-struck stamp (Fig. 77, No. 2).

Middle Saxon Imported Pottery
by Catherine Coutts
Four sherds of the rare 'Tating' ware were found, in separate contexts. Three of these were adjoining, and form part of the base and wall of a single vessel. The other sherd, a handle, was banded with stripes in the characteristic manner of 'tin-foil' decoration.

Another import, a small sherd of oxidised pottery with rouletted decoration was also found, in a residual context.

The pottery fragments were analysed macroscopically with the aid of a ×20 binocular microscope and then carefully thin-sectioned: the results are as follows.

Tating ware handle (Fig. 77, No. 3, context *709*, spit of brown soil in the area of the graveyard; co-ordinate 211.22/517.12)
This handle fragment has a highly burnished black surface (Munsell colour: 2.5YR 3/0 black), and had been decorated with three lines of tinfoil of which vestigial traces remain. Two lines run across, and the third line runs down the extreme right-hand side of the face of the handle. The core of the shshed is a light brownish-grey (Munsell colour: 2.5YR 6/2), and has some small inclusions of black iron-ore and limestone visible. The form of the handle — an 'S' shape, flatted on one side and rolled on the other — bears a strong resemblance to the Hamwic example illustrated in Hodges (1981, 16, fig. 3,1,2). The thin-sections of the two handles suggest that they are in fact the same fabric. The thin-sections of the Middle Harling sherd (TS 153 Coutts 1992, 361) and the Hamwic sherd (Hodges T-SP 81) reveal optically anisotropic light brown clay matrices, with abundant, well-sorted inclusions of sub-angular quartz crystals at 0.05–0.25mm across, plus a few larger crystals at 0.4–0.5mm across. There is also a light scatter of iron ore present at *c.* 0.05mm across, and a few additional fragments at 0.5–1.0mm across.

Tating ware base fragment (Fig. 77, No. 4, context *198*, filling of bone pit *197*; post-hole *428*, Building B; context *522*, spit in brown soil over Building B and ditch *700*)
The joining three sherds that make up the base fragment were undecorated, or more accurately, no traces of tinfoil were visible; however, the basal quarter of Tating ware pitchers are frequently undecorated (see for example the Tating ware pitcher from Birka — Hodges 1982, 59, fig. 10). The surface was highly burnished, with visible lines of polish (Munsell colour of the surface: 2.5YR 3/0), with a light brownish-grey core (Munsell colour: 2.5YR 6/2), the same as the handle described above. Thin-sectioning revealed an optically anisotropic light grey-brown clay matrix, with abundant, sub-angular crystals of quartz ranging from 0.05–0.25mm across, plus a few larger composite crystals at *c.* 0.4mm across. In addition there was a light scatter of iron ore at *c.* 0.05–0.2mm across. It appears that the handle and base fragments are from the same vessel.

The oxidised sherd (Fig. 77, No. 5, layer *187*, post-medieval ditch *854*)
The small size of this sherd makes it difficult to provenance accurately. It is a reddish yellow colour with mica visible on the surface and no other apparent inclusions (Munsell colour: 5YR7/6). The fragment bears a resemblance to a group of sherds from Ipswich, but unfortunately the identification of these sherds is at present tentative. Thin-section reveals a red-brown optically anisotropic clay matrix with a dense scatter of quartz crystals at *c.* 0.05–0.1mm across, plus a few larger crystals of sub-angular quartz at 0.4–0.5mm across. In addition, numerous small (0.2–0.3mm long) laths of muscovite are visible, and a few fragments of iron ore at *c.* 0.5mm across. Under thin-section this sherd appears dense and gritty, which compares well with those from Ipswich. Burnishing on one of the Ipswich fragments suggests that the sherds belong to Hodges Class 21. A Rhenish centre is postulated as the source of this pottery type.

The two pottery types described above occur infrequently in Carolingian-period sites throughout northern Europe. On the continent Tating ware appears to be most common in the so-called emporia — Dorestad, Ribe, Kaupang, Birka and so on — whereas in England, apart from its appearance in Hamwic, York, Wharram Percy and London, its distribution seems to be predominantly confined to East Anglia. Whether this is due to recovery biases, or is a reflection of the pottery's distribution, is difficult to say, but the high number of Tating-free Middle Saxon sites in the Hamwic-Hampshire area suggests the latter: this pottery type, along with other Rhenish wares, found its principal 'market' in East Anglia.

Late Saxon
Of 1369 sherds over 83% (1141 sherds) are of Thetford-type ware, 16% St Neots-type ware (226 sherds) and less than 1% (2 sherds) Stamford ware.

Thetford-type Ware
Most of this is in a standard hard grey fabric, and might have been made in Thetford. However, the proportion of flat bases (32% of the total) is larger than that at Thetford. On the Brandon Road site (Dallas 1993) only 7% of Thetford ware bases were flat. Some of the Thetford-type ware from Harling must therefore have been produced at

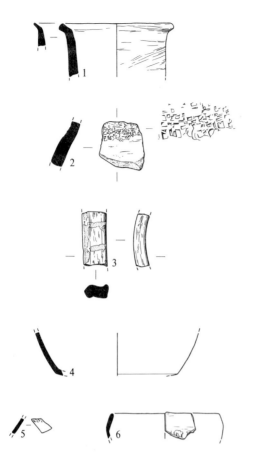

Figure 77 Pottery nos 1–6. Scale 1:4;
stamp no. 2, Scale 1:2.

other centres. Jar or 'cooking pots' comprised the main form (113 rims) with only three bowl rims present. Spouted pitchers are indicated by five spout fragments and three handles. Eighteen sherds derive from storage jars, the majority of which are in a coarse and often flaky fabric. There is one flange fragment, possibly from a lid. Three sherds carry an incised wavy line, and rouletted decoration occurs on thirty-two sherds. In twenty-seven cases a diamond pattern and in the rest a squarish design is employed.

St Neots-type Ware
The variation in colour and texture is similar to those from Thetford (Rogerson and Dallas 1984, 123). Twenty-nine rims are from jars or 'cooking pots' and only two from bowls (both of inturned profile). All bases are sagging. There is no decoration present.

Stamford Ware
by Kathy Kilmurry
Form, glaze and fabric types have been classified according to Kilmurry 1980. A body sherd with shallow horizontal grooving in Fabric B with exterior glaze 6 from the filling of a post-medieval bone pit is dated *c.* 1150–1200. A possibly distorted rim from a small ovoid vessel (Fig. 77, No. 6), probably Form 19–03, in Fabric A, is covered with Glaze 4 on both surfaces, and carries a fragment of stamped decoration (M12). Found in filling over the junction of ditches *139* and *611*, this example is unusual in that this form is normally undecorated (Kilmurry 1980, 18). It is dated *c.* 900–1025.

Medieval
A total of 1359 sherds of medieval pottery was recovered. Included within this figure are sherds of Early Medieval ware. Although rim forms enable this ware to be distinguished from fully medieval coarse ware, Early Medieval body and basal sherds are, to the writer who has not conducted any detailed fabric analysis, insufficiently different from later wares to warrant separation. Small jars (form a) in Dallas' (1984, 123) fabric (i) are common, as are larger jars (form b) in fabrics (i) and (ii). There is a solitary ginger jar (form c) and very few bowls (d). Fabric (i) is the most common, but fabric (ii), a harsh pimply ware, occurs more frequently at Harling than at Thetford. It is unusual in Norfolk except in the Thetford-Harling region and appears to have West Suffolk origins. The majority of medieval pottery is in the equivalent of Dallas' fabric (i) but tends to be reduced, and lacks the brownish/reddish blotchiness so characteristic of the Early Medieval ware; bodies are normally wheel-thrown. Elaborately 'moulded' rims of high medieval type (as, for example, Jennings 1981, fig. 15) are absent from this excavation.

In the absence of detailed work on the Early Medieval/medieval unglazed wares from the site no catalogue is published. The lack of study also makes illustration undesirable. Because so few curfews or firecovers from the region have been published, a fine example from this site (Fig. 78) deserves to be an exception.

Thirty-nine sherds, many joining, of a **curfew** (Fig. 78, No. 7) in hard sandy fabric with sparse quartz inclusions up to 1mm diameter; grey core with brown surfaces; sooting on underside of dome; stub of handle with circular stabbed hole; multiple circular vent-holes in dome; at least three semi-circular holes in wall; applied strip above rim on exterior; four rows of incised wavy line decoration. Contexts *4, 105, 125, 130, 452, 457, 464, 465, 517* and *554,* topsoil, spits in brown soil in south-east area, spit over pits *500, 589, 600* and *610,* and fillings of pits *500* and *589.*

The glazed earthenware assemblage is small, but exceptional. Of forty-one sherds, thirty-four (83%) are of Hedingham-type ware, four of Grimston ware, two of Late Medieval and Transitional Ware (Jennings 1981, 61–2), and one with rounded white inclusions and possibly a Cambridgeshire product. The scarcity of Grimston ware (1% of the glazed ware) contrast with its frequency (65% of the glazed ware) at Ford Place Thetford, a site occupied throughout the 13th and 14th centuries (Dallas 1993). The medieval site north of the excavation, known from surface evidence only (context *7*) has produced a 'normal' quantity of Grimston glazed ware; it is the dominant medieval glazed ware. The non-Hedingham-type wares from the excavation, all from unstratified contexts, may derive from this site to the north, while the Hedingham-type pieces, almost all from the south-east part of the excavation in stratified and unstratified contexts, result from occupation on the excavated site. The date of this occupation surely ended earlier than that at Mill Lane Thetford and context *7*. The dating of the Hedingham-type ware is discussed below by Carol Cunningham, but a cessation of activity on the excavated site by *c.* 1250 seems most likely in view of the scarcity of glazed Grimston ware and the absence of developed forms in medieval coarseware.

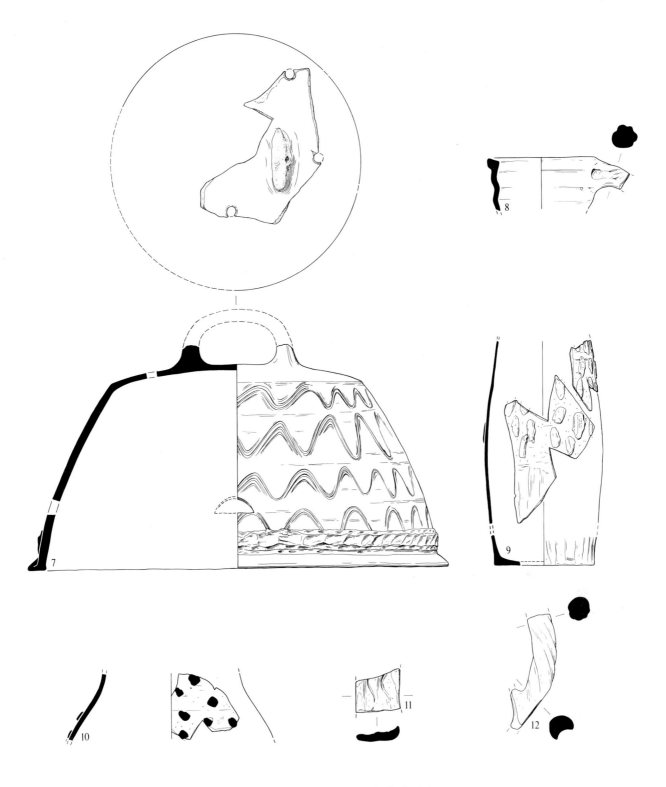

Figure 78 Pottery nos 7–12, Scale 1:4.

Hedingham-type Ware

by Carol Cunningham

Out of this group of thirty-four sherds, twenty-nine are Hedingham fineware. The fabric is smooth, fine and fairly soft, uniformly orange-brown or pink-buff. Its most distinctive inclusion is fine white mica, but it also contains quartz, and a little iron ore, clay pellets and altered glauconite.

Figure 78, No. 8 has a triangular, thickened rim and a twisted rod handle with deep finger-impression on either side, and a partial clear glaze. It has one very small applied pellet in contrasting white clay. Slightly sandy light orange fabric with very sparse mica. (Context *544*, spit in south-east area).

Another jug (Fig. 78, No. 9) is probably conical, and is covered, at least on the upper body, with fairly roughly applied pads in the body clay, under a clear glaze with occasional green patches. (Contexts *4, 105, 125, 337, 457* and *554*, topsoil, spits in brown soil in south-east area and filling of pit *589*). A sherd from a slightly sagging, knife-trimmed base may belong to the same vessel. (Context *125*, spit over pits *500, 589, 600* and *610*).

Figure 78 No. 10 survives only as body sherds from a more globular jug. It has small thick applied pellets in a contrasting clay to the body, appearing dark brown under the glaze. This jug is unusually reduced, giving a harder grey exterior surface in places with an olive green glaze. Some of the fragments are also painted with a dark red slip, perhaps forming a band of lattice decoration. (Contexts *4, 100, 105, 133, 464, 465* and *554*, topsoil, basal filling of ditch *138* and spits in brown soil in south-east area).

A fragment of strap handle (Fig. 78 No. 11) has incised decoration under a light olive green glaze. (Context *4*, topsoil). Another fragmentary body sherd (context *153*, spit in brown soil in north-west area) has cream slip under a clear glaze.

The kilns at Sible Hedingham, in northern Essex between Colchester and Saffron Walden (TL 783 322), were excavated in 1971 and 1972 (Webster and Cherry 1972, 205; 1973, 184), but are at present unpublished. Their products are found throughout the northern half of Essex, southern Cambridgeshire and sporadically in Norfolk (North Elmham, Wade 1980b, 452; Thetford, (Rogerson and Dallas 1984, 124–5). Its apparent absence in Suffolk may be resolved when further work is carried out. Its presence here, therefore, is unusual but not unprecedented.

The best study of this industry arises from the large groups from excavations at Colchester (Cotter forthcoming). There the fineware is present by the middle of the 12th century or soon after. Its development closely follows that of London ware until near the middle of the 13th century, during which time it is the dominant fineware throughout the northern half of Essex, although not occurring widely beyond there. At Chelmsford it was supplanted by Mill Green ware around the middle of the 13th century.

A second, smaller group displays many of the same characteristics, but in a distinctly coarser, sandier fabric with almost no mica. Fig. 78.12, for example (context *408*, filling of ditch *700*) has the same twisted rod handle: another sherd in the same fabric has applied dark brown pellets (context *560*, spit in brown soil north of ditch *604*). Coarsewares were produced at Hedingham (Webster and Cherry 1972, 205), and it may be that this included decorated jugs.

XII. The Terracotta Panel
(Fig. 79)
by Paul Drury

This fragment was found in a rabbit disturbance by Mr Bert Reeve of East Harling some years before 1980, close to the north edge of Church Clump, a few yards west of the south-west corner of the excavations. This spot must have been very close to the site of St Andrew's Church marked by the Ordnance Survey.

The panel is in a slightly pinkish-buff hard fabric, tempered with much very fine sand and some larger inclusions of flint, ironstone and part-fired clay up to *c.* 10mm in diameter. It appears to have been moulded in the usual way, with some enhancement of the face after turning out. The back shows strike marks, and some deep scoring due to the dragging of larger inclusions. The right-hand edge is wavy and appears to have been knife cut whilst the piece was green, which accords with this edge falling short of the centre-line of the design. The face

retains traces of a thin coating of white limewash, the back of brownish buff lime mortar.

The top edge has a projecting (and much damaged) rather flat ogee moulding, above blind tracery (developed on the inset) in two planes. Both the cusped heads to the subsidiary panels, and, apparently, the enclosing frame, are distinctly round-headed. The piece probably comes from the side of a tomb chest, although other possibilities exist, for example the base of a screen of masonry rather than wood.

It is the round heads of the panels, as well as the material, which makes this object distinctive. Round-headed subordinate lights and panels occur in later perpendicular work (*e.g.*, Harvey 1978, 224), but fully round-arched tracery appears but rarely in eastern England during the later 15th century, for example on a brick overmantel from Prittlewell, Essex (Lloyd 1925, 384), which is of distinctly Flemish inspiration. Many of the terracotta windows at Sutton Place, Sussex, of *c.* 1521–33 have cusped round heads (Lloyd 1925, 144–5, 417). This forms an apposite parallel because of the common material, which enjoyed a brief vogue in the 1520s. However, in East Anglia terracotta of this date (rather than moulded brick at, *e.g.*, East Barsham, *c.* 1520–3), at Layer Marney Hall and in the associated series of East Anglian tombs (Baggs 1968) was essentially renaissance in its details. The panel from Middle Harling raises the intriguing possibility that there was either a gothic component to the output of this workshop, or, more likely, an earlier (late 15th/early 16th century) workshop producing material which, because of its superficial resemblance to sandstone, may be more widespread than is currently realised.

XIII. Human Bone
by Rosemary Powers

The Cemetery
Because of the pressures of time, very little of the cemetery area was excavated. Only those burials which overlay earlier ditches were removed. In view of the intrinsic interest of accompanied Late Saxon burial *451*, the bones were retained and submitted for examination.

Burial *451*
The skull fragments were mislaid. This deprives us of the main source of information. The long bones are very pitted from soil erosion and most are not measurable. They are:
Humeri. Both shafts, lacking ends.
Ulnae. Both shafts, one retaining part of the proximal end.
Radii. Both shafts, the right retaining the distal end.
Femora. Shafts of both femora, the right retaining a little knee.
Tibia. The left is complete, the right lacks the knee. Tib length = 381mm. Estimated stature is male 174cm.
Eroded fragments of innominates, the sex is probably male. Lower part of normal sacrum.

Bone Pit *167*
[Of the contents of large numbers of bone pits emptied, those from only one pit have been selected for examination. The remaining bones have been reburied.]

Four skulls were complete enough to see in the photograph *in situ*, but nine more were pieced together from fragments not necessarily bagged together. It could

Figure 79 Terracotta panel fragment. Scale 1:4.

not be assumed that pieces in the same bag belonged to the same individual. Far less could it be assumed that post-cranial elements belonged to particular skulls. Some very fresh, unstained breaks were noticed but the missing pieces were not present in the collection. The mandible count showed only one juvenile but the long bones and their size differences made eight the minimum figure, the youngest individual being about three years. A maxilla belonging to a seven-year-old is also present. Most of the bones are male, but at least one skull is clearly female, fine and thin almost like a juvenile but the sutures are matured. The few innominate bones complete enough to sex showed five male to four female, and a detached pubis shows parity trauma indicating that the woman had had children. A few of the long bones were complete enough to measure and estimate stature upon, but because they were mainly tibiae, the sex was not certain. Taken as males three femora give 172cm, 160cm, 170.4cm respectively. Six right tibiae give 165cm, 174cm, 157cm, 174cm, 170cm, 173.5cm. Trotter and Gleser's (1958) formula was used. There is no evidence of fresh trauma, disease, sword cuts or fracturing, so it cannot be said how they died.

The count on the skulls was eleven skulls, which together with eight frontal bones, make nineteen adults (none metopic) but the count on the femora assigning two per person arbitrarily (assessing which side was impractical in many cases due to damage) gives

thirty-eight adults; the children were counted separately. Together they give a minimum of forty-six. The dearth of small bones suggests that this was a secondary interment.

The cranial index ranged from 71 to 83. The dental wear was flat. This combination of flat wear and relatively good general health looks Saxon. They range from childhood to old age and complete tooth loss.

Anomalies
There was only one case of cribra orbitalis among the skulls, moderate in degree. No cases of cribra femoris were noted as this region was so frequently damaged. Although the teeth are quite heavily worn — 4 to 6 on Brothwell chart — there is considerable caries, as follows:

Number of teeth with caries 7 upper, 3 lower = 10 out of total possible 44 upper, 49 lower = 93 (mostly interproximal caries).

Number of teeth lost in life 22 upper, 52 lower = 74 out of total possible 103 upper, 180 lower = 283.

One edentulous jaw skews the frequency. Number of abscesses 4 upper, 1 lower = 5.

At least one adult had an unusually thick skull, and another had a mass of wormians around lambda, but their skulls cannot be reconstructed.

Calvarium number eleven had a healed wound on the orbital ridge, penetrating to the endocranium but not causing death or infection. Its upper border looks like a healed sword cut below which is a circular hole with healed edges. The lower border has broken away recently. (Hole 13 mm wide, cut 25mm long).

One lumbar five vertebra found among the post-cranial bones has the arch detached with a false joint, a condition called spondylolysthesis. Another, normal, lumbar five was found also.

Two of the femora had markedly osteoarthritic femur heads, with ebernation and ulceration. While not exactly similar in shape they may form a pair. A very osteoarthritic elbow joint (ulna and radius) is also present.

One humerus shows a supra-condylar exostosis (a harmless rare oddity).

XIV. Animal Bones

Animal bones were hand collected from all contexts below the topsoil where they were present. Out of a total weight of 185.5kg, 77.8% was found in the removal of spits in the brown soil below topsoil and above the natural subsoil. Although much of this brown soil was in fact the upper filling of cut features, in particular ditches, the method of excavation prevented the finds therein from being assigned with confidence to individual features. This material has not been retained. From the filling of cut features came a total of 41.1kg (22.2%). As the date range of the contexts ranges from Middle Saxon (or earlier) to post-medieval, and as there were no great concentrations of bone in any period, the material has been retained but not analysed.

XV. Mollusca

Of 626 oyster shells recovered, 228 (26.5%) were from sealed contexts, with the remainder from spits in the brown soil below topsoil and above the natural subsoil. Notable concentrations were in the filling of the western end of the possibility Middle Saxon ditch *139/661*, in the filling of slot *146* in medieval Building D, and in uppermost layers of medieval pits *500, 589, 600* and *610*. Small quantities of mussel shells were found in three medieval contexts and one unstratified, while a solitary cockle shell was recovered from a Late Saxon or earlier shallow scoop (*412*). Land snail shells, which were ubiquitous, were collected during excavation. They have not been studied.

Chapter 4. Conclusions

I. The Prehistoric Occupation

The Late Neolithic pit clusters at Middle Harling were found accidentally in the course of a project designed to understand the deposition of a coin hoard of the 8th century AD. In these circumstances their significance in the settlement pattern of Breckland is not overwhelming. Frances Healy has stressed the importance of surface flint resources in the region, and the contents of several pits, along with the large quantity of knapping debris from later contracts supports her suggestion. This site's riverine location is matched by other known settlement sites in Breckland, a zone where excessively well-draining subsoils make the availability of surface water a leading factor in site location.

Healy enquires whether similar results would be forthcoming from other comparably sited excavations in the region. Certainly such small-scale and presumably 'episodic' sites as this are most likely to be encountered fortuitously. Their visibility on the ground or from the air is limited, and in Breckland in particular they are masked on the surface by a veritable carpet of struck flint which may not be related in any observable way to sub-surface features. Neolithic and Bronze Age settlement sites will continue to be excavated as a by-product of research on other more visible classes of site, often post-prehistoric in date. In 1989, for example, excavation immediately outside the 10th century AD town defences at London Road, Thetford, revealed, amongst an absence of Saxon finds and features, a cluster of over twenty Iron Age pits which contained residual Neolithic and Bronze Age material (Davies 1993). Further afield, at Spong Hill, North Elmham, a similar prehistoric spin-off occurred, but this time on a project aimed at the 5th–6th centuries AD and with results for prehistory on an altogether more massive scale (Healy 1988).

With the exception of a lone late Bronze Age awl (Fig. 52, no. 134) signs of late prehistoric activity are absent from the excavated site and its immediate surrounds, and there is no hint of influence from the nearby early Iron Age type-site at Micklemoor Hill. The late Iron Age is represented by a gold-plated base metal stater from *c.* 100m south west of Church Clump (coin no. 70).

II. The Roman Period

A thin scatter of pot sherds from the excavation must represent manuring, predominantly in the first half of the Roman period. There were no features certainly of this date, and of the coins, half were probably post-Roman imports to the site.

III. The Early Saxon Period

The almost complete absence of evidence for activity between the 5th and 6th centuries in and around the excavation is noteworthy. Perhaps the area had reverted to pasture serving settlements some distance away, with arable farming around a contemporary settlement returning only in Middle Saxon times. This would fit the evidence derived from local pollen analysis (Murphy 1984, 15).

IV. The Middle Saxon Period

'In practice, the long tradition of British fieldwork by excavation has produced a huge number of partially dug sites...' (Champion 1978, 207). The Middle Harling excavation has certainly added to this list, as the surface spread of Ipswich-type ware (*c.* 1.3 hectares), far exceeding the area of excavation (*c.* 1300m^2) clearly indicates (Fig. 4). However, complete excavation was never the intention behind the project whose primary aim was the 'setting in context' of the Beonna Hoard. By a combination of surface collection and partial excavation this has been achieved. A first stage in an understanding of the Hoard is an appraisal of the Middle Saxon settlement of Middle Harling within the East Anglian Kingdom.

Fieldwork in central Norfolk (Wade-Martins 1980b, 84) and more recently in south-east Suffolk (Newman 1989) has shown that evidence for Middle Saxon settlement sites is readily available, in the form of Ipswich-type ware sherd scatters, on the ploughed surfaces of East Anglian fields, often but not always in intimate proximity with medieval churches. Middle Harling is typical in this respect and other examples can be seen on Fig. 2 at Bridgham, Larling, Eccles and Knettishall. Despite wide variations in the quantity of Ipswich-type sherds in different parts of the Kingdom (compare Norfolk Marshland (Rogerson and Silvester 1986) with north-east Norfolk (Lawson 1983, 70–2)), it is likely that fieldwalking could locate Middle Saxon pottery scatters in the majority of parishes where the land was available for survey. To date Ipswich-type ware has been recorded in 161 out of 543 modern civil parishes in Norfolk (excluding central Norwich). Middle Harling is not the only site of this date in Harling parish but it is the largest, unlike the others near a church, and the only one yet to have produced contemporary metal objects.

Metal detecting since the mid-1970s has added a large number of find-spots to the map of Middle Saxon East Anglia. Many of these spots are on sites with pottery, others are apparently stray finds of coins, metalwork or both. No site has yet been subjected to both rigorous fieldwalking and systematic detecting. It is early days and our body of data is still 'meagre in content and eccentric in distribution' (Carver 1989, 143). However, it is already clear that sites appearing very similar in terms of their pottery assemblages can yield metal artefacts of widely differing quality and quantity.

Unfortunately no other sites close to Middle Harling have been systematically surveyed, but it is possible to compare the site with others in Norfolk and Suffolk.

Middle Harling does not appear as a top-ranking site where metalwork is concerned, but it is definitely above average. The pins, the 9th-century strap-ends, and other pieces such as the cruciform mount fragment (Fig. 45 No. 86) are of high quality and prolific, even if the number of objects from the excavated area itself was small. Other artefact types, however, are absent, for example elaborately decorated hooked tags, 'caterpillar' or ansate brooches, styli and pins with interlace-decorated heads (Hinton 1990, 61). Some sites for example Barham, Suffolk (Newman forthcoming) and Bawsey, Norfolk (Blackburn et al. forthcoming) have a later 7th-century component in their metalwork matched by the occurrence of primary scatters. There are no such finds from Middle Harling, and the coin series does not start before c. 750.

The Harling Ipswich-type assemblage is standard, and is an exact visual match to material from Ipswich itself (P. Blinkhorn pers. comm.). Its quantity is somewhat greater than from many rural sites. On the other hand the presence of pottery in the Tating ware tradition does mark out Middle Harling as potentially exceptional, none of the other three find-spots in Norfolk being on 'normal' sites: North Elmham, an episcopal settlement (Hodges 1980), West Dereham, a probable monastic site, and Brancaster, a Saxon Shore fort (Hodges 1985).

The physical location of Middle Harling appears unremarkable, and it is not situated on an island or near-island as are 'high status' and probably monastic sites such as Bawsey, Brandon (Carr et al. 1988) and Burrow Hill, Butley (Fenwick 1984). Nor is it in a close relationship with a major Roman town as is the numismatically prolific site at Caistor St Edmund. Harling, then, is an above-average Middle Saxon site in terms of its artefacts, is topographically undistinguished, and has produced no evidence that it was occupied early in the period, i.e. in the later 7th century.

The position of Middle Harling in the hierarchy of both local and East Anglian Middle Saxon settlement will only be assessed with any accuracy after further archaeological work in three areas: a sub-regional survey of Norfolk and Suffolk and Breckland similar to that carried out by John Newman (1989) in south-east Suffolk; small and large scale excavation of 'poor' and 'productive' sites throughout the East Anglian Kingdom; excavation of a greater area at Middle Harling itself. On this latter point it should be noted that a mere c. 10% of the area of pottery scatter (including Church Clump) has been examined. Keith Wade when assessing the large-scale excavations at Wicken Bonhunt, Essex complained of '...the problems of attempting to interpret a settlement with the evidence from only half of it.' (Wade 1980, 102). Middle Harling's Middle Saxon status may still be uncertain, but it is distinguished by its Beonna Hoard, to which we will now turn.

No part of the Hoard was found in situ. Of fifty-one coins from the excavated site, twenty-five were recovered from the topsoil and underlying brown soil over an area measuring 6m by 2.3m (Fig. 9). This 'epicentre', with its long axis east-to-west, straddled the line of the north wall of Late Saxon building B. The cache might first have been disturbed by any of the cut features in the area, ditch 23 being a likely candidate. Subsequent dispersal may have resulted from the digging of other features and from ploughing (a medieval plough iron was found on the site, Fig. 69 No. 106). This dispersal was largely northwards, with only three Beonna coins being found to the south of northing 530 (Fig. 9). Three more (Fig. 33 Nos 614,

652–3) from the field north of the excavation may be unrelated to the Hoard or may have been fortuitously incorporated into some minor transportation of soil. It is difficult to believe that the three southern outliers (Fig. 33 Nos. 58, 709 and 714) were ever part of the Hoard.

There is no certainty about the role that sceattas may have played in the Hoard's composition. Their distribution was somewhat different from that of the Beonnas (Fig. 9). Two out of the seven from the excavation (28%) were found south of northing 530, in contrast to only 0.58% of the Beonnas. No sceattas came from north of the excavation but three occurred to the south (Fig. 33, Nos 82, 615 and 711). This pattern suggests that, if some sceattas were once part of the Hoard, others were not, and that both classes of coin were in normal use on the site.

The original receptacle of the Hoard is of course unknown. It may have been very small. At the Coroner's inquest in 1982, thirty-six new half-pence coins (similar in size to Beonna pennies) were shown to fit into a standard-size matchbox. Thus even if a total of 100 coins had been secreted, a container of no more than 70 cubic cm would have been necessary. Although such a container may have been of wholly perishable material, it is tempting to speculate whether the coins had been hidden in either the Tating ware vessel (Fig. 78, Nos 3 and 4) or in a box of wood or leather decorated with repoussé copper alloy strips (Fig. 45, Nos 88–93). The imported pot was perhaps too large, so the box, whose 8th-century ornamental binding strips were found in many fragments in the general area of the hoard, is a more likely candidate. In this context it is worth recalling the Lurk Lane Beverley hoard of twenty-three mid 9th-century stycas. The coins had been secreted in a tiny ?leather purse and buried next to a T-junction of paths. Discovered under meticulously archaeological conditions, the containing feature was the most ephemeral of scoops (Armstrong et al. 1991, 13–4).

It is quite reasonable to suggest that someone hand-digging a post-hole or ditch would not have noticed the coins in a distintegrated container as he shovelled them out. By 1980/1, and presumably many centuries earlier, the Beonnas had become dull in colour, encrusted with sand, and very difficult to distinguish with the naked eye amongst the soil.

When the location of the Hoard within the settlement area is considered, the evidence for Middle Saxon activity in the excavation is disappointingly slight, with the earliest recorded building being of the 10th century. There were no Middle Saxon pits, and only four stretches or fragments of ditches may have been of this date. It could be claimed that over 130 potsherds from so small an area, along with quantities of metalwork, should point to occupation on this spot. However, more than seventy sherds and more numerous metal objects collected from the surface of, rather than from excavation in, the field south of Church Clump show that it was there that the main zone of Middle Saxon settlement must have been situated.

Whether a church and/or cemetery lay north of this main area in the 8th or 9th centuries is not known. It seems probable that accompanied burial 451, of the later 9th or early 10th century and perhaps of an intrusive Dane, would have been placed on the edge of an existing cemetery. The insertion of Scandinavian, or Scandinavian influenced burials into churchyards is not unknown (Graham-Campbell 1980; Morris 1983, 61). This burial was dug into ditch 652 which may have been a northern boundary to the graveyard. To the north of this ditch lay an area, not occupied but strewn with an amount of domestic refuse, close to the main part of the settlement but separated from it by a cemetery. In this peripheral location a suitable place was chosen for the secretion of the Hoard.

On the placing of the Hoard in relation to the settlement one final point must be made. With the current difficulties of narrowing the date range of Ipswich-type ware to less than the long span from earlier 7th century to *c.* 900, it is possible that all this type of pottery at Middle Harling might post-date the deposition of the Hoard. The same later dating might apply to most of the metalwork. It is conceivable then, but very unlikely, that the Hoard was buried at a place near which there was little or no contemporary human settlement.

As important as the original position and container of the Hoard are the political, military or economic circumstances which led to its assembly and burial. Marion Archibald (1985, 33–4) has discussed what is known of the political upheavals in East Anglia under Mercian hegemony in the mid-8th century. Detail of this period is as incomplete as King Beonna is shadowy, so we cannot point to any event that may have provoked the Hoard. Although there is, as has been already stressed, still much to learn from archaeology about the hierarchy of Middle Saxon settlement in the area, the geographical position of Middle Harling and its proximity to certain other places may have some bearing on this problem. As suggested by Miss Archibald (1985, 30) the moneyer's name EFE may be found in the place-name Euston, a parish 6km to the south-west in Suffolk (Fig. 80). Neighbouring Euston on the east is Coney Weston, surely a Middle Saxon royal centre (Scarfe 1972, 96–7). Kenninghall lies 6km east of Middle Harling. Ekwall (1960, 272) gives a personal name *Cyne* or *Cena* as the first element in this name. It is surely possible that *Cyning* is an acceptably plausible alternative derivation, and that here we have another Middle Saxon royal centre. The place was certainly a royal vill at the Conquest, with a network of soke rights owed to it by the freemen of many surrounding vills. Amongst these was Ulfketel's manor identified with Middle Harling. Thetford, 11km west-south-west of Middle Harling, was put forward by Marion Archibald (1985, 30) as a potential site for the minting of the Efe coins, although at that time archaeological evidence for Middle Saxon occupation there was scant (Fig. 80). Salvage recording during by-pass construction in 1988 produced coin, metalwork and pottery evidence for an 8th-9th century settlement just to the north-west of the Late Saxon town. This settlement was apparently much larger than a normal rural site. The new evidence was augmented by trial excavations in 1990 (SMR no. 24849). Royal associations of a slightly post-Beonna date may also be claimed for another nearby place, Larling, 4.5km to the north (Fig. 80). Here the church is dedicated to St Aethelbert, king of East Anglia, who died in 794. Near the church was found a decorated whale bone panel which carries the representation of the She-wolf and twins. By an unusual coincidence, as Barbara Green has noted (1971, 323), this motif occurs on a coin of the same Aethelbert. Interestingly, another nearby church is dedicated to St Aethelbert. This is the parish church of East Wretham, lying *c.* 8.5km north-west of Middle Harling. Although the proximity of two royal vills, a moneyer's vill, a semi-urban mint and two churches with

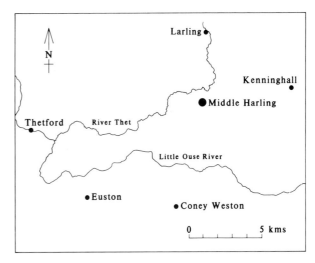

Figure 80 Map showing locations of Middle Harling and other nearby places of definite or probable significance at the time of the deposition of the Beonna Hoard.

slightly later royal associations would not add any specific detail to the circumstances of the Hoard, a strong degree of royal interest in this part of the Norfolk-Suffolk border does seem difficult to deny. This indicates a range of possibilities that the imaginative reader may wish to pursue.

Finally, it should be noted that in 1993 a Beonna coin, moneyer EFE, was found at Eccles in Quidenham parish (SMR no. 29883; see Fig. 2).

V. The Late Saxon Period

Whatever the true date of the change-over from Ipswich-type to Thetford-type ware, the mid-9th century or nearer 900, we are on stronger ground at Middle Harling when we reach the 10th century with plentiful evidence, timber buildings, ditches, and artefacts, taking the occupation of the excavated area on into the Conquest period. This occupation covered all of the excavation except for the south-east part occupied by the cemetery, although a broad band across the centre had been removed by medieval ditches. Late Saxon pottery dominated in all parts of the site bar the south-east where it was eclipsed by medieval material (Fig. 81). Finds of metalwork were most numerous over the eastern half (Fig. 12). As with the Middle Saxon, no clearly defined industrial activity is evidenced by the finds, apart from textile production (spindle-whorls, comb teeth, and loomweights) and perhaps woodworking. The former was an activity common to most Saxon settlements, rural and urban. Metal finds, the box mounts (Fig. 46) and finger rings (Fig. 38) may point to some degree of wealth as do the coins, usually rare as individual losses on rural sites; eight coins ranging from Berhtwulf to Edward the Confessor provide remarkably even coverage of the 200 years beginning in the mid-9th century.

The two buildings with near complete plans (A and B) are of very similar size (*c.* 97 and 100m^2 internally) and of similar proportions, both being approximate double squares. They were of somewhat different construction, at least so far as the fixing of upright members in the ground is concerned. Building A, with its post-in-trench

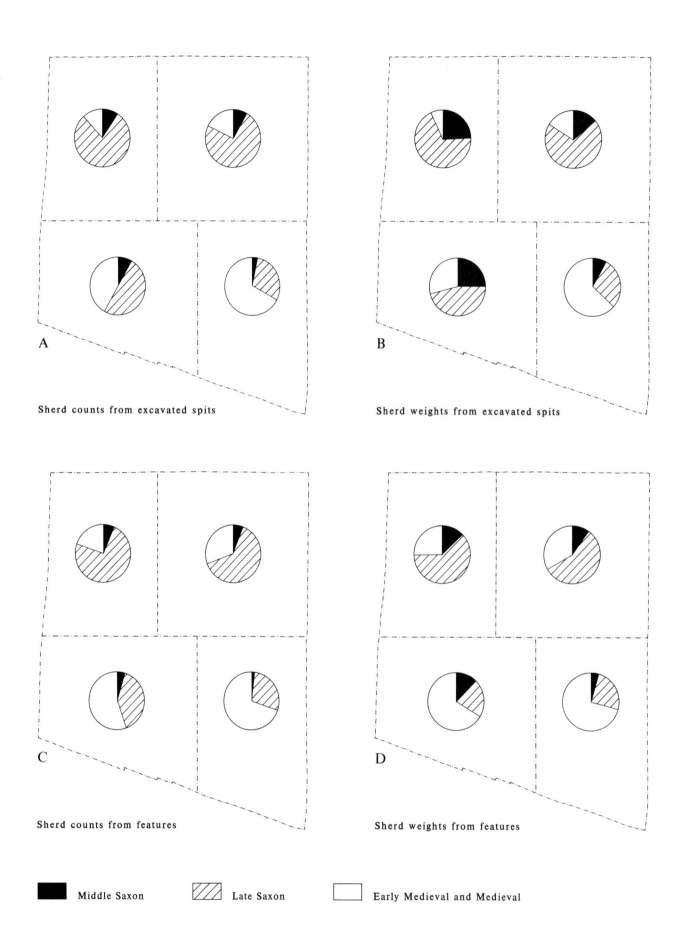

Figure 81 Pie-charts showing proportions of Middle Saxon, Late Saxon and medieval pottery in four subdivisions of the excavated area, from excavated spits of brown subsoil and from features, by sherd counts and by weights.

construction, lacked evidence for the end walls which were presumably non-loadbearing, while B had unevenly spaced post-holes of differing depths along four walls, with evidence of rebuilding or repair particularly in the western wall (repair is more plausible than the use of staggered posts, as in James *et al* 1984, fig. 9b). Neither building has a convincing entrance position, although the interruption midway along the southern wall of building A might indicate a doorway. The remains of a hearth survived within B, but otherwise there was no evidence of flooring or function. If clay had been used for flooring then some trace of it would have been recovered in the soil within the areas of the structures.

VI. The Medieval Period

The occupation within the excavated area continued through the late 11th and 12th centuries, becoming restricted to the south-east part of the site where buildings D and F were situated south of a complex of pits, probably dug for the disposal of cess and domestic rubbish. Medieval pottery predominated here, and 79.9% of the medieval sherd total was recovered from this area.

A broad east-to-west swathe was cut through the centre of the excavation by a series of medieval ditches. It is regrettable that, despite much time and effort spent in recording their courses and in cutting sections across them, their functions remain uncertain. The extent outside the excavated area of these ditches is also uncertain, and could only be traced by geographical survey or further excavation; no cropmark evidence has yet been recorded. Although in the western part some ditches can be seen as successive phases of a northern boundary to the graveyard along with a stable eastern boundary represented by ditch *611*, at least three (*138, 604* and *852*) continued north-eastwards, away from the graveyard. Here, perhaps, they formed a shifting boundary on the north side of the property which contained buildings D and F.

This property which was only partially uncovered in the excavation, was intensively occupied, with a succession of buildings and the only group of pits on the site. The status of the property is uncertain, and the finds, with the exception of the silver seal matrix (Fig. 44 No. 81) are of no help in this matter. The seal matrix of Jeffrey de Furneaux was recovered in topsoil over the north-west corner of the property. The first Jeffrey de Furneaux was lord of the manor of Middle Harling in *c.* 1180 (Blomefield 1805, 313–4). His second son, another Jeffrey, was also lord and had died by 1234. The latter must have been the seal's owner; according to Blomefield he was the first de Furneaux to reside at Harling and John Cherry suggests a date in the first half of the 13th century. Perhaps, then, we are dealing here with part of a manorial complex lying to the east of the parish church.

On pottery evidence the property was abandoned as an occupation site around the mid-13th century. The inhabitants may have moved to a new site, just to the north (context *7*, Fig. 4) or elsewhere. This move was either part of the decline of Middle Harling which has been shown to have been well under way by 1334 (Davison 1980), or another example of the Norfolk phenomenon of settlement relocation from church town to common edge in the period between the Conquest and the mid-14th century. A manorial site need be no less prone to movement in the 13th century than a peasant holding.

Enough has been written above about the small size of the excavation in relation to the surface indications of Middle Saxon settlement to show that further excavation, particularly in the area south of Church Clump, would be very desirable. However, once again an intensive examination of a restricted piece of ground has been carried out in the midst of a largely unstudied landscape. To focus on 'sites' has long been the concern of most archaeologists and perhaps will remain so. Middle Harling's environs are better understood than many areas, but long after this report has gathered dust, fieldwork in Harling and surrounding parishes may well give the data contained herein added significance.

Bibliography

Archibald, M.M., 1985 — 'The coinage of Beonna in the light of the Middle Harling Hoard', *Brit. Numis. J.*, 55, 10–54

Armstrong, P., Tomlinson, D. and Evans, D.H., 1991 — *Excavations at Lurk Lane Beverley, 1979–82*, Sheffield Excavation Reports 1

Ashley, S., Penn, K. and Rogerson, A., 1991 — 'A further group of Late Saxon mounts from Norfolk', *Norfolk Archaeol.* 51, 225–9

Atkin, M., Carter, A. and Evans, D.H., 1985 — *Excavation in Norwich 1971–1978, Part II*, E. Anglian Archaeol. 26

Babelon, E., 1902 — *Histoire de la Gravure sur gemmes en France*, (Paris)

Backhouse, J., Turner, D.H. and Webster, L., (eds), 1984 — *The Golden Age of Anglo-Saxon Art*, (British Museum, London)

Baggs, A.P., 1968 — 'Sixteenth-century Terracotta Tombs in East Anglia', *Archaeol. J.* 125, 297–301

Bailey, M., 1989 — *A marginal economy?: East Anglian Breckland in the later Middle Ages*, (Cambridge)

Bamford, H.M., 1985 — *Briar Hill Excavation 1974–1978*, Northampton Development Corporation Archaeological Monograph 3

Bennett, K.D., 1983 — 'Devensian Late-Glacial and Flandrian vegetation history at Hockham Mere, Norfolk, England. I. Pollen percentages and concentrations', *New Phytol.* 95, 457–87

Blackburn, M., Rogerson, A. and Margeson, S., forthcoming — 'A productive Middle and Late Saxon site at Bawsey, Norfolk' in Metcalf, D. M. and Blackburn, M. (eds), *Productive sites of the Middle Saxon Period: Proceedings of the 12th Oxford Symposium on coinage and monetary history*, Brit. Archaeol. Rep. (London)

Blomefield, F., 1805 — *An essay towards a topographical history of the county of Norfolk* Volume I, (London, 2nd edition)

Briscoe, G., 1954 — 'A Windmill Hill site at Hurst Fen, Mildenhall', *Proc. Cambridge Antiq. Soc.* 47, 13–24

Briscoe, G., 1957 — 'Swale's Tumulus: A combined Neolithic A and Bronze Age Barrow at Worlington, Suffolk', *Proc. Cambridge Antiq. Soc.* 50, 101–112

Buckton, D., 1986 — 'Late 10th and early 11th-century *cloisonné* enamel brooches', *Medieval Archaeol.* 30, 8–18

Burleigh, R., Hewson, A., Meeks, N., Sieveking, G. and Longworth, I., 1979 — 'British Museum natural radiocarbon measurements X', *Radiocarbon* 21, No. 1, 41–7

Capelle, T., 1968 — *Der Metallschmuck von Haithabu*, (Neumünster)

Carr, R.D., Tester, A. and Murphy, P., 1988 — 'The Middle-Saxon settlement at Staunch Meadow, Brandon', *Antiquity* 62, 371–377

Carver, M., 1989 — 'Kingship and material culture in early Anglo-Saxon East Anglia' in Bassett, S., (ed), *The Origins of Anglo-Saxon Kingdoms*, (London)

Champion, T., 1978 — in Cherry, J.F., Gamble, C. and Shennan, S. (eds), *Sampling in contemporary British Archaeology*, Brit. Archaeol. Rep. 50, 207–225, (Oxford)

Chautard, J., 1871 — *Imitations des monnaies au type Esterlin*, (Nancy)

Clark, J.G.D., 1934 — 'Derivative forms of the *petit tranchet* in Britain', *Archaeol. J.* 91, 34–58

Clark, J.G.D., 1960 — 'Excavations at the Neolithic site at Hurst Fen, Mildenhall, Suffolk', *Proc. Prehist. Soc.* 26, 202–245

Clarke, D.L., 1970 — *Beaker pottery of Great Britain and Ireland*, (Cambridge)

Clarke, H. and Carter, A., 1977 — *Excavations in King's Lynn 1963–1970*, Soc. Medieval Archaeol. Monograph Ser. No. 7, (London)

Clarke, D.V., Cowie, T.G. and Foxon, A., 1985 — *Symbols of Power at the Time of Stonehenge*, (Edinburgh, National Museum of Antiquities of Scotland)

Clarke, W.G. and Hewitt, H.D., 1914 — 'An early Norfolk trackway: the "Drove" Road', *Proc. Prehist. Soc. East Anglia* 1 (iv), 427–34

Cleal, R., 1984 — 'The Later Neolithic in eastern England' in Bradley, R. and Gardiner, J., (eds), *Neolithic studies. A review of some current research*, Brit. Archaeol. Rep. 133, 135–158 (Oxford)

Clough, T.H. McK. and Cummins, W.A. (eds), 1988 — *Stone axe studies volume 2*, Counc. Brit. Archaeol. Res. Rep. 67 (London)

Corbett, W.M., 1973 — *Breckland Forest soils*, Soil Survey of England and Wales Special Survey 7 (Harpenden)

Cotter, J., forthcoming — *Post-Roman pottery from excavations in Colchester, 1971–85*, Colchester Archaeol. Rep. 7

Coutts, C.M., 1992 — *Pottery and the Emporia: imported pottery in Middle Saxon England with particular reference to Ipswich*, (unpubl. PhD thesis, University of Sheffield)

Dallas, C., 1993 — *Excavations in Thetford by B.K. Davison between 1964 and 1970*, E. Anglian Archaeol. 62

Davies, J.A., 1993 — 'Excavation of an Iron Age pit group at London Road, Thetford, 1989', *Norfolk Archaeol.* 41, 441–61

Davis, R.V., 1985 — 'Implement petrology: the state of the art — some problems and possibilities' in Phillips. P. (ed), *The archaeologist and the laboratory*, Counc. Brit. Archaeol. Res. Rep. 58, 33–35 (London)

Davison, A.J., 1980 — 'West Harling: a village and its disappearance', *Norfolk Archaeol.* 27, 295–306

Davison, A.J., 1983 — 'The distribution of medieval settlement in West Harling', *Norfolk Archaeol.* 28, 329–336

Demay, G., 1877 — *Inventaire des sceaux des Artois*, (Paris)

Demay, G., 1881 — *Inventaire des Sceaux de la Normandie*, (Paris)

Dymond, D.P., 1973 — 'The excavation of a prehistoric site at Upper Chamberlain's Farm, Eriswell', *Proc. Suffolk Inst. Archaeol.* 33(1), 1–18

Ekwall, E., 1960 — *The Concise Dictionary of English Place-Names,* (4th edition, Oxford)

Ellis, B., 1984 — 'Spurs' in Rogerson, A. and Dallas, C., *Excavation in Thetford 1948–59 and 1973–80',* E. Anglian Archaeol. 22

Evison, V.I., 1977 — 'An enamelled disc brooch from Great Saxham', *Proc. Suffolk Inst. Archaeol.* 34, 1–13

Fell, C.I., 1951 — 'A Late Bronze Age urnfield and Grooved Ware occupation at Honington, Suffolk', *Proc. Cambridge Antiq. Soc.* 45, 30–43

Fenwick, V., 1984 — 'Insula de Burgh: excavations at Barrow Hill, Butley, Suffolk, 1978–81', *Anglo-Saxon Stud. Archaeol. Hist.* 3, 35–54

Fingerlin, I., 1971 — *Gürtel des hohen und späten Mittelalters,* (Berlin)

Ford, S., forthcoming — 'Report on the excavation of a Neolithic ring ditch and Roman features at Manor Farm, Lower Horton, Berkshire'

Gell, A.S.R., 1949 — 'Grooved Ware from West Runton, Norfolk', *Antiq. J.* 29, 81

Godwin, H. and Tallantire, P.A., 1951 — 'Studies in the Post-Glacial history of British vegetation. XII. Hockham Mere, Norfolk', *J. Ecol.* 39, 285–307

Goodall, A.R., 1982 — 'Objects of copper alloy' in Coad, J. and Streeten, A., 'Excavations at Castle Acre Castle, Norfolk, 1972–1977', *Archaeol. J.* 139, 138–301

Goodall, A.R., 1984 — 'Non-ferrous metal objects' in Rogerson and Dallas 1984, 68–75

Goodall, I.H., 1984 — 'Iron objects' in Rogerson and Dallas 1984, 76–106

Goodall, I.H., 1993 — 'Iron buckles and personal fittings' in Margeson, S., *Norwich Households,* E. Anglian Archaeol. 58, 32–33

Graham-Campbell, J., 1980 — *Viking Artefacts A Select Catalogue,* (London)

Graham-Campbell, J., 1982 — 'Some new and neglected finds of 9th century Anglo-Saxon ornamental metalwork', *Medieval Archaeol.* 26, 144–151

Green, B., 1971 — 'An Anglo-Saxon Plaque from Larling, Norfolk', *Antiq. J.* 51, 321–3

Green, E.B., 1980 — 'Two 9th-century silver objects from Costessey', *Norfolk Archaeol.* 37, 351–353

Green, H.S., 1980 — *The flint arrowheads of the British Isles,* Brit. Archaeol. Rep. 75 (Oxford)

Hall, R., 1984 — *The Viking Dig,* (London)

Hart, C.R., 1966 — *Early Charters of Eastern England,* (Leicester)

Harvey, J., 1978 — *The Perpendicular Style,* (London)

Healy, F., 1984a — 'Farming and field monuments: the Neolithic in Norfolk' in Barringer, C. (ed), *Aspects of East Anglian prehistory (twenty years after Rainbird Clarke),* 77–140 (Norwich)

Healy, F., 1984b — 'Recent finds of Neolithic Bowl pottery in Norfolk', *Norfolk Archaeol.* 39, 65–82

Healy, F., 1985 — 'The struck flint' in Shennan, S.J., Healy, F. and Smith, I.F., 'The excavation of a ring-ditch at Tye Field, Lawford, Essex', *Archaeol. J.* 142, 177–207

Healy, F., 1986 — 'Struck flint' in Petersen, F.F. and Healy, F., 'The excavation of two round barrows and a ditched enclosure on Weasenham Lyngs, 1972' in *Barrow Excavations in Norfolk, 1950–1982,* E. Anglian Archaeol. 29, 80–89

Healy, F., 1988 — *The Anglo-Saxon cemetery at Spong Hill, North Elmham, Part VI: Occupation during the 7th to 2nd millennia BC,* E. Anglian Archaeol. 39

Healy, F., 1992 — 'Lithic material', 'Pre-Iron Age pottery' and 'Pre-Iron Age activity' in Gregory, T., *Excavations in Thetford, 1980–82, Fison Way,* E. Anglian Archaeol. 53, 143–147, 148–154, 188

Healy, F., 1993 — 'The struck flint' in Chowne, P., Healy, F. and Bradley, R., 'The excavation of a Neolithic settlement at Tattershall Thorpe, Lincolnshire' in Bradley, R., Chowne, P., Cleal, R.M.J., Healy, F. and Kinnes, I., *Excavations on Redgate Hill, Hunstanton, Norfolk and at Tattershall Thorpe, Lincolnshire,* E. Anglian Archaeol. 57, 93–105

Henig, M. and Heslop, T.A., 1986 — 'Three 13th century seal matrices with intaglio stones in the Castle Museum, Norwich', *Norfolk Archaeol.* 39, 305–309

Herne, A., 1988 — 'A time and place for the Grimston bowl' in Barrett, J.C. and Kinnes, I.A., (eds), *The Archaeology of Context in the Neolithic and Bronze Age: Recent Trends,* (Sheffield, Department of Archaeology and Prehistory), 9–29

Hinton, D.A., 1990 — *Archaeology, Economy and Society: England from the fifth to the fifteenth century,* (London)

Hodges, R., 1980 — 'Characterisation and discussion of identified important sherds' in Wade-Martins 1980a, 424–426

Hodges, R., 1981 — *The Hamwih Pottery: the local and imported wares from 30 years' excavations at Middle Saxon Southampton and their European context,* Counc. Brit. Archaeol. Res. Rep. 37

Hodges, R., 1982 — *Dark Age Economics: the origins of towns and trade AD 600–1000,* (London)

Hodges, R., 1985 — 'An unusual (?) Tating ware vessel' in Hinchliffe, J., with Green, C.S., *Excavations at Brancaster 1974 and 1977,* E. Anglian Archaeol. 23

Hook, D., La Nièce, S. and Cherry, J., 1988 — 'A 15th century mercury-silvered buckle from Hillington, Norfolk', *Antiq, J.* 68, 301–305

James, S., Marshall, A. and Millett, M., 1984 — 'An Early Medieval Building Tradition', *Archael. J.* 141, 182–215

Jennings, S., 1981 — *Eighteen centuries of pottery from Norwich,* E. Anglian Archaeol. 13

Kilmurry, K., 1980 — *The Pottery Industry of Stamford, Lincolnshire c. A.D. 850–1250,* Brit. Archaeol. Rep. 84 (London)

Lawson, A.J., 1983 — *The Archaeology of Witton, near North Walsham, Norfolk,* E. Anglian Archaeol. 18

Lawson, A.J., 1986 — 'Notes on three Norfolk barrow excavations at Bridgham, Cockley Cley and Old Hunstanton' in Lawson, A.J., *Barrow excavations in Norfolk, 1950–82,* E. Anglian Archaeol. 29, 104–110

Leaf, C.S., 1935 — 'Report on the excavation of two sites in Mildenhall Fen', *Proc. Cambridge Antiq. Soc.* 35, 106–27

Legge, A.J., 1981   'The agricultural economy' in Mercer, R.J., *Grimes Graves, Norfolk, excavations 1971–72: Volume I*, 79–103 (London)

LLoyd, N., 1925   *The History of English Brickwork*, (London)

LMMC   *London Museum Medieval Catalogue*, 1940, (London)

Longworth, I.H., 1971   'The Neolithic pottery' in Wainwright, G.J. and Longworth, I.H., *Durrington Walls: excavations 1966–1968*, Rep. Res. Comm. Soc. Antiq. London, 29, 48–155

Longworth, I.H., 1981   'Neolithic and Bronze Age pottery' in Mercer, R.J., *Grimes Graves, Norfolk, excavations 1971–72: volume I*, 39–59 (London)

Longworth, I.H., Ellison, A.B. and Rigby, V., 1988   'The Neolithic, Bronze Age and Later', *Excavations at Grime's Graves, Norfolk 1972–6 fascicule 2*, (London, British Museum)

Manby, T.G., 1974   *Grooved Ware sites in Yorkshire and the north of England*, Brit. Archaeol. Rep. 9 (Oxford)

MacGregor, A., 1985   *Bone Antler Ivory and Horn. The Technology of Skeletal Materials since the Roman Period*, (London)

Margary, I.D., 1973   *Roman Roads in Britain*, (London, 3rd ed.)

Margeson, S.M., 1982   'Viking period trefoil brooches', *Norfolk Archaeol.* 38, 208–210

Margeson, S.M., 1986   'A group of Late Saxon mounts from Norfolk', *Norfolk Archaeol.* 39, 323–327

Margeson, S.M. and Williams, V., 1985   'The Artefacts' in Ayers, B., *Excavations within the North-East Bailey of Norwich Castle 1979*, E. Anglian Archaeol. 28

Mårtensson, A.W., 1976   *Uppgrävt förflutet för Pkbanken ï Lund* Archaeologica Lundensia, 7

Martin, E.A., 1979   'Grooved Ware sherds from West Stow', *Proc. Suffolk Inst. Archaeol. Hist.* 34, 205–6

Martin, E.A., Plouviez, J. and Feldman, H., 1986   'Archaeology in Suffolk 1985', *Proc. Suffolk Inst. Archaeol. Hist.* 36, 139–56

Miket, R., 1976   'The evidence for Neolithic activity in the Milfield Basin, Northumberland' in Burgess, C. and Miket, R., (eds), *Settlement and economy in the third and second millennia B.C.*, Brit. Archaeol. Rep. 33, 113–142 (Oxford)

Morris, R., 1983   *The church in British archaeology'*, Counc. Brit. Archaeol. Res. Rep. 47

Murphy, P., 1984   'Environmental archaeology in East Anglia' in Keeley, H.C.M., *Environmental Archaeology: A regional review*

Musty, J., Wade, K. and Rogerson, A., 1973   'A Viking pin and inlaid knife from Bonhunt Farm, Wicken Bonhunt, Essex, *Antiq. J.* 53, 287

Newman, J., 1989   'East Anglian Kingdom survey-final interim note on the south east Suffolk pilot field survey', *Bull. Sutton Hoo Res. Comm.* 6, 17–19

Newman, J., forthcoming   'Barham, Suffolk — Middle Saxon market or meeting-place?' in Metcalf, D.M. and Blackburn, M. (eds), *Productive sites of the Middle Saxon Period: Proceedings of the 12th Oxford Symposium on coinage and monetary history*, Brit. Archaeol. Rep. (London)

North, J.J., 1975   *English Hammered Coinage, Vol. 2 Edward I to Charles II 1272–1662*, (London)

North, J.J., 1980   *English Hammered Coinage, Vol. 1 Early Anglo-Saxon to Henry III c. 600–1272*, (London)

Oman, C., 1974   *British Rings 800–1914*, (London)

Øye, I., 1988   'Textile Equipment and its working environment, Bryggen in Bergen c. 1150–1500', *The Bryggen Papers*, vol. 2, (Norwegian University Press)

Pearson, G.W. and Stuiver, M., 1986   'High-precision calibration of the radiocarbon time scale, 500–2500 BC', *Radiocarbon* 28, 839–862

Pearson, G.W., Pilcher, J.R., Baillie, M.G.L., Corbett, D.M. and Qua, F., 1986   'High-precision C-14 measurement of Irish oaks to show the natural C-14 variations from AD 1840–5210 BC', *Radiocarbon* 28, 911–934

Peers, C. and Ralegh Radford, C.A., 1943   'The Saxon Monastery of Whitby', *Archaeologia* 89, 27–88

Piggott, S., 1931   'The Neolithic pottery of the British Isles', *Archaeol. J.* 88, 67–158

Piggott, S., 1954   *The Neolithic cultures of the British Isles*, (Cambridge)

Pitts, M.W., 1978   'Towards an understanding of flint industries in Post-Glacial England', *Univ. London Inst. Archaeol. Bull.* 15, 179–97

Pryor, F., 1978   *Excavation at Fengate, Peterborough, England: the second report*, Royal Ontario Museum Archaeology Monograph 5 (Toronto)

Pryor, F., 1984   *Excavation at Fengate, Peterborough, England: the fourth report*, Northamptonshire Archaeological Society Monograph 2, Royal Ontario Museum Archaeology Monograph 7

Rigold, S.E. and Metcalf, D.M., 1977   'A check list of English finds of sceattas', *Brit. Numis. J.* 47, 31–52

Robinson, P., 1992   'Some Late Saxon Mounts from Wiltshire', *Wilts. Archaeol. Nat. Hist. Mag.* 85, 63–69

Roesdahl, E., 1992   *From Viking to Crusader*, (Sweden)

Rogerson, A. and Dallas, C., 1984   *Excavations in Thetford 1948–59 and and 1973–80*, E. Anglian Archaeol. 22

Rogerson, A. and Silvester, R.J., 1986   'Middle Saxon occupation at Hay Green, Terrington St. Clement,' *Norfolk Archaeol.* 39, 320–322

Saville, A., 1981a   'The flint and chert artefacts' in Mercer, R.J., 'Excavations at Carn Brea, Illogan, Cornwall, 1970–73', *Cornish Archaeol.* 20, 101–152

Saville, A., 1981b   *Grimes Graves, Norfolk, excavations 1971–72: Volume II the flint assemblage*, Department of the Environment Archaeological Reports 11 (London)

Sawyer, P.H., 1968   *Anglo-Saxon Charters: an annotated list and bibliography*, (London)

Scarfe, N., 1972   *The Suffolk Landscape*, (London)

Sims, R.E., 1978   'Man and vegetation in Norfolk' in Limbrey, S. and Evans, J.G., (eds), *The effect of man on the environment: the Lowland Zone*, Counc. Brit. Archaeol. Res. Rep. 21, 57–62 (London)

Smith, I.F., 1956   'The decorative art of Neolithic ceramics in south-east England and its relations' (unpubl. Ph.D. thesis, Univ. of London)

Smith, I.F., 1965   *Windmill Hill and Avebury,* (Oxford)

Smith, I.F., 1974   'The Neolithic' in Renfrew, C. (ed.), *British prehistory a new outline,* 100-36 (London)

Smith, I.F., 1979   'The chronology of British stone implements' in Clough, T.H. McK. and Cummins, W.A. (eds), *Stone axe studies,* Counc. Brit. Archaeol. Res. Rep. 23, 13–22

Smith, R.A., 1915   'Pottery, worked bones and worked chalk' in Clarke, W.G. (ed.), *Report on the excavations at Grime's Graves, Weeting, Norfolk, March-May 1914,* 208–17 (London)

Stewart, I.H., 1967   *The Scottish Coinage,* (revised ed. with supplement, London)

Thompson, F.H., 1960   'The deserted medieval village of Riseholme, near Lincoln', *Medieval Archaeol.* 4, 95–108

Tonnochy, A.B., 1952   *Catalogue of Seal-dies in the British Museum,* (London)

Trotter, M. and Gleser, G.C., 1958   'Re-evaluation of Estimation of Stature based on Measurement of Stature taken during Life and Long Bones after Death', *Amer. J. Phys. Anthrop.* 16, 79–123

Wade, K., 1980a   'A settlement site at Bonhunt Farm, Wicken Bonhunt, Essex' in Buckley, D.G. (ed.), *Archaeology in Essex to AD 1500,* Counc. Brit. Archaeol. Res. Rep. 34, 96–102 (London)

Wade, K., 1980b   'The Pottery' in Wade-Martins 1980a, 413–477

Wade-Martins, P., 1980a   *Excavations in North Elmham Park 1967–1972,* E. Anglian Archaeol. 9

Wade-Martins, P., 1980b   *Village sites in Launditch Hundred,* E. Anglian Archaeol. 10

Wainwright, G.J. and Longworth, I.H., 1971   *Durrington Walls: excavations 1966–1968,* Rep. Res. Comm. Soc. Antiq. London 29 (London)

Wainwright, G.J., 1972   'The excavation of a Neolithic settlement on Broome Heath, Ditchingham, Norfolk, England', *Proc. Prehist. Soc.* 38, 1–107

Waterman, D.M., 1959   'Late Saxon, Viking and Early Medieval finds from York', *Archaeologia* 97, 59–106

Webster, L. and Backhouse, J. (eds) 1991   *The Making of England,* (British Museum, London)

Webster, L.E. and Cherry, J., 1972   'Medieval Britain in 1971', *Medieval Archaeol.* 16, 147–212

Webster, L.E. and Cherry, J., 1973   'Medieval Britian in 1972', *Medieval Archaeol.* 17, 138–188

West, S.E., 1963   'Excavations at Cox Lane (1958) and at the town defences, Shire Hall Yard, Ipswich (1959)', *Proc. Suffolk Inst. Archaeol.* 29, 233–303

Weyman, J., 1985   'Flint and agate' in Miket, R., 'Ritual enclosures at Whitton Hill, Northumberland', *Proc. Prehist. Soc.* 51, 141

Whitelock, D., 1930   *Anglo-Saxon Wills,* (Manchester)

Whittle, A., 1981   'Later Neolithic society in Britain: a realignment' in Ruggles, C.L.N. and Whittle, A.W.R. (eds), *Astronomy and society in Britain during the period 4000–1500 B.C,* Brit. Archaeol. Rep. 88, 297–342 (Oxford)

Williamson, G.C., 1967   *Trade tokens issued in the seventeenth century Vol. 2,* (London)

Wilson, D.M., 1964   *Anglo-Saxon Ornamental Metalwork 700–1100 in the British Museum,* (London)

Wilson, D.M., 1965   'Late Saxon metalwork from the Old Minster, 1964', *Antiq. J.* 45, 262–4

Index